Tommy and I
Together as one

By Marc Richardson
Psychic Medium

DEDICATION

I would like to dedicate this book to all my wonderful family.
I love you all.

Thank you for standing by me, and for being there whenever I have
needed you.

Especially:

My amazing wife, best friend, and soul mate, Mel,
I love you more than words can say,
Always and Forever x x

Lauren and Luke – I am so proud of you both and love you so much x

Mum – Thank you for being you, and for being an inspiration in all I have
done and achieved in my life.

Let me not forget;
Nan "Molly", Dubs, Paul, Jo, Flea, and my two beautiful nieces. x

Also remembering with love and affection those who have passed

Grandad "Grumps", Ena, Cyril and Peter

Until we meet again
x

Contents

Some of the names in this book have been changed to keep the anonymity of those concerned, as all readings carried out by Marc are in the strictest of confidence. The usage of any parts of any readings mentioned in this book has had the prior consent of those people involved.

Foreword

My name is Marc Richardson; I was born on 21st April, 1970, and was brought up in East Sussex, on the South Coast of England, along with my younger brother and sister.

After many conflicting career choices including a few seasons as a Redcoat / compare for Butlins, training at Eastbourne catering college to be a chef, and a few other failed attempts as a salesman, I finally settled with running my own transport and warehousing business based in the countryside near Lewes, just a few miles outside the seaside resort of Brighton, in East Sussex.

Following a severe road traffic accident as a pillion passenger on a motorcycle, at the tender age of 13, I was hospitalised for over 12 months, and spent many more months recuperating after that.

During the numerous major operations I had at such a young age, I had, many of what I now know to be "out of body experiences" which I can still vividly recall.
On one particular day I was honoured and privileged to be connected with my now inseparable spirit guide "Tommy", whom from that day to this has guided and taught me about this world, the afterlife and about sharing my knowledge with others.

I have dedicated myself to do this ever since.

I have literally been involved in "spiritual work" from a very young age. I have travelled extensively throughout the world, read, learnt and studied many methods of practice, and have witnessed many true phenomena, some of which neither I myself nor science can explain!

I am a great believer in positive thought and positive attitude and believe we can all make a difference to our own lives, by finding our inner self and or spirit guide(s).

"A positive thinker sees the invisible, feels the intangible, and achieves the impossible".

Now today working from my base in East Sussex, I am continuously fully booked with private readings, courses and events allowing me to share my knowledge, to many people looking for either a verified connection with loved ones who have passed, or to those who are looking for a new direction in their life.

More increasingly I am giving speeches and lectures to those who just want to learn more about this very thought-provoking gift, which I have honed since the age of 14.

I am also lucky enough to work alongside some of the UK's leading paranormal groups, investigating paranormal activity in many of the UK's leading "haunted" locations, such as Michelham Priory, in East Sussex and The Galleries of Justice, Nottingham.

I have also more recently undertaken exploration investigations in the Somme region of Western France, and Bastogne in Belgium.

Having appeared in several newspaper and magazine articles regarding my work, in 2009/10, I was nominated for a Spiritual Award alongside psychic Tony Stockwell. It was a true honour for me just to be nominated in the same category as him.

So a very big thanks you to all of you who voted for me on that occasion.

After being fortunate and privileged enough to meet so many wonderful people, and after being asked many questions over and over again, I decided to set myself a challenge to write this book, not only to answer those questions I most often get asked, but also to offer my knowledge and understanding, to those people who really are interested in developing their own personal psychic gift, awareness of the afterlife, or spiritual connections.

So, believing entirely in positive thought now comes the hard part. Having never actually written a book, it does currently seem like a daunting idea, and if nothing else a great challenge!

Currently I do not know anything about writing a book let alone getting one published. So if you are now sitting down reading this as a book, something went right, and in that case I am very grateful that you have decided to read it, so thank you.

The other main reason for me writing this book is because Tommy my spirit guide says that I should, and as I believe unequivocally in what he is telling me, I am taking a chance that he knows what is right on this occasion as well.

So with positive thinking and a head full of stuff, here I go!

Chapter One - How it all began.

I can without doubt remember every single minor detail of the entire day, every tiny thought that entered my head, every feeling and emotion that swept over me during what would shortly turn out to be the most life changing day ever!

I had been away camping at a Cub Scout weekend not too far from where we were now living, as I had done many times before, with all my regular scouting friends, the year was 1983. I was just 13 years old. I originally joined the group as young a Cub and then advanced onto the Junior Scouts because I loved the outdoor activities we were able to participate in, and the structure it gave me was something I thoroughly enjoyed, principally because it was my ultimate dream, when I was old enough without question, to join the Army.
This was something I wanted to do so much, all I talked about was joining the army and serving my country, and for me the closest I could get at that time of my young life was by being in the scouts.

Even though my family had just recently moved out of the local area from where my scout group was based, my parents continued to allow me attend the same cub scout group that I had done for many years previously, and they constantly drove me to and from the group every week, which was a round trip distance of approximately 20 miles or so.

The camping weekend had been booked and organised several weeks before, and everyone was so excited about going on it. I made sure my name was down on the list as soon as it was announced, and I even helped my parents pay the fees for the weekend, by saving up pocket money which I would earn from doing chores, just so that I could attend it.

There was something special about being away at the camp, when all us boys were all together were a team. We all loved the outdoors, being away from our families and learning new skills.

I was so excited when the day finally came and everyone met at the scout hut HQ, ready to load and board the mini bus and van which would be taking us and our equipment on the trip.
Even if it was just a few miles down the road and only for three days, it felt like we were going away for ever. From the moment we left the HQ until arriving at the camp we couldn't wait for the adventure to start.

The whole weekend was great fun; we learnt how to build shelters, light fires and we even had to cook our own meals. The worst part was that we also had to learn how to wash and clean up afterwards!

It was a really bright, sunny day when I awoke, early on the final morning of this particular camping weekend. The sunshine was streaming through the side of the canvass tent where eight of us laid like sardines in our sleeping bags. Once we had heard the booming scoutmaster's voice calling us we all very quickly emerged from the tent, some of us still wearing the clothes from the day before.

We all took a brisk early morning run around the field we were staying in, as we did every morning and no excuses were allowed, and then we went straight into the freezing cold showers, which were made up of two oil drums full of cold river water, set up on a platform above our heads.
Then it was business as usual we all had plenty of things to do before we could actually go home on that day.
Following a hearty breakfast cooked by ourselves, like clockwork, it all began to happen. We had tents to take down, fold and pack away, pots and pans to clean and scrub and then finally everything had to be packed back into the mini bus and the van, which along with all of us cubs and scouts was a military operation on its own.
Everyone had a job to do and a place to be.

As the packing up began it suddenly became evident to our scout master that there were two vehicles to get back to our starting location, and only one driver, (as the other driver had been taken home ill the night before). Our scout leader came up with the answer; he was going to have to primarily take everyone home in the mini bus, and then afterwards return for the van, on his motorbike.

He would then place the motorbike in the back of the second van to finally drive home, and finish his day.
Therefore when loading the van we had to ensure we left enough room for his motorcycle to be added in later in the day.

Being that I now lived the furthest distance away than any of the other kids, from our current HQ location, it was suddenly announced by my scout leader, out of the blue, that to make things even easier for him, I would be coming back with him on the back of his motorcycle as a pillion passenger, so that once we had retrieved the van he could then take me home directly afterwards.

I have to be very honest and say, this idea was something which I was really not expecting, and nor was I very excited about, even though many of my scouting friends said they thought it would be a thrilling end to the great weekend we had all just shared.

Nevertheless despite my nervousness, my scout leader confirmed his choice was me, and he reiterated the reason for it. Reflecting on it now many years later, whist writing this, I really had no other option. Obviously I couldn't really say anything to the scout master, as he was the person in charge, the person I looked up to, and I had to get home as my parents were expecting me later in the day. I also did not want to say to him in front of all my friends about the fact that I didn't really want to go on the motorbike, it as they may have thought that I was being silly, and in the scouts we were all "tough guys" well in front of each other anyway!

It is funny the things you do remember, but I distinctly recall, that once I had been given the news, my mood change to one of being a little quiet and maybe anxious, but not only that, at the same time I specifically remember so did the weather change, it became overcast, grey and cold, something which has always stuck with me.
My mood became like that of the weather!

On the initial journey back to the scout hut HQ, all of us boys were loaded into the mini bus, along with our own luggage and some of the camping equipment which we had managed to squeeze into any available gap, including our laps. So that enough room had been left in the van.

The main conversation of all my friends the entire journey back was about how lucky they all thought I was at being able to go on the scoutmaster's motorbike, and some even offered to swap with me.

Keeping a brave face I just smiled at them.

Once we had returned every one of my friends home safely, we headed directly for the scoutmaster's home, to collect his motorbike ready for the return journey to the campsite, where we would then collect the van, and I would finally be taken home the 25 miles or so to my parents, who would be waiting for me to return.

From the moment I was told I felt very anxious about having to go on the back of the motorbike, maybe it was because it was my first time ever on the back of a motorbike, and maybe also because my parents didn't even know about it. I kept wondering what they would say when they found out.
Whatever was causing my anxiety, I knew something wasn't right, and I knew in my mind that something was going to happen.
It was a strange feeling which I had never felt or experienced before in my young life, and however much I tried to dismiss it in my mind, the feeling was right back over and over, stronger and louder in my head.

Arriving at the scoutmaster's home he parked the mini bus up against his garage door, and once he had unlocked and opened the garage up I finally got to see for the first time the motorbike I was going to be travelling on.
Again my memory is very clear, I remember thinking that the motorbike was a lot different to what I had imagined it to be. It was not as new looking or as shiny as the one I had mentally pictured, in my mind all morning, but even still it was a motorbike, and more to the point I knew as I stood there looking at it, that very shortly I would be on it.

First things first, we had to unload all the remaining equipment from the mini bus into the garage for storage until it was needed again.
Several times as we unloaded the van I kept thinking that I must tell the scout master how I was actually feeling, but every time I tried the words just wouldn't come out of my mouth.

I just knew that the situation wasn't right from the cold feeling I kept getting creeping over me, and the mild knotting of my stomach, but what could go wrong? It was one small journey I kept telling myself. That's all.

Once the unloading of the mini bus was completed my scout master handed me what looked like a very old crash helmet to wear, it was dark blue in colour with no visor and it obviously didn't really fit me correctly.
I could move my head quickly in one direction and the helmet would then go the other way, but at least once my scout leader had helped me to do the strap up as tight as possible, it stayed on my head!

It was only at this point that something actually triggered inside me and I finally plucked up the courage, (now I wasn't with my mates and the trip was imminent), to tell my scout leader about my nervousness and anxiety, which by now was growing so rapidly that I could hear my pulse pounding fast in my ears, inside the helmet.
However he reassured me that as long as I sat up straight, kept still, and that I held on to him tight, nothing could possibly go wrong.
 "I have done this many times before with others from the group". He reminded me,
"Everything will be fine, and the journey is not that long, maybe 20-25 minutes".
Again something just really didn't ring right in my mind about the journey that I was just about to undertake, and the feelings I had were not going away.

Almost immediately and without any time to waver, I was on the back half of the seat, and the motorbike left our starting location with me on the rear as the pillion passenger, we were off heading for our destination.
I was so apprehensive as the motorbike moved swiftly through the local traffic, and having no visor on the crash helmet meant that I could feel the wind against my skin, and I am sure this probably made it seem like the motorbike was going even faster than it actually was.

We were now less than 8 miles to our final destination. I was holding on tighter than tight to the rider controlling the motorbike, a person I had to trust, not wanting to move or shift my weight at all.

As instructed, I sat there rigid, sometimes just closing my eyes as we came to a corner.

With the limited view I had from the old and slightly too large crash helmet, I was nervously trying to "enjoy" the new experience which my friends and I had discussed not an hour before, but each and every time I tried the same heavy, strong feeling just kept rushing back into my head and stomach.
Something was going to happen; I just knew it. I could feel the blood pumping around my body faster and faster, and the thumping of my pulse in my ears, I could have at that point actually cried.

Every now and again I would open my eyes as much as I could with the wind on my face, rapidly attempting to assess the road ahead trying to be ready for the next bend or obstacle that I could see coming up in the distance.
Then I realised, the one thing that I could see ahead of us was a railway crossing that we were fast approaching, with cars speeding over the old rails crossing the pitted main road. I suddenly recalled all the times that when as a family we had gone over this very same crossing in our car, the car would shake and shudder from side to side.

Maybe I should hold on tighter at this point I thought to myself, so as we approached the railway crossing I did just that, I closed my eyes, tucked my head down behind the scout master and held on so firmly. The motorbike certainly did bounce a bit as we crossed the undulating rails, but within seconds we were over it and continuing our journey. Again I specifically remember giving out a large sigh of relief once we had gone over the crossing. Maybe, just maybe that was the part of the journey that I had been so subconsciously nervous about?

Gaining speed and momentum we now had less than 5 miles to go and were nearly there, most of the journey from that point was straight forward, after the next fast approaching bend, the road was virtually straight right up to our final destination, and as far as I was concerned, then and only then I would be the home and dry.

But still no matter how quickly we were getting through the journey and how much I was trying to enjoy this adventure, the feeling had still not gone away, all I knew was that I wanted this journey over and

I wanted it over as soon as possible. My brain was now finding it so hard to separate all of the emotions I was feeling, especially the one of "something is going to happen" to me.

Then it did.

The motorbike abruptly and unexpectedly hit a very large pot hole which was located on the side of the road. With an enormous jolt, jump and shudder, I felt an incredible nudge as the bike lifted and swayed, and then I felt one very large quick sharp pain followed after by nothing but a flapping sensation. I knew something had happened to me but couldn't tell what.

I instantaneously started to feel weak, fragile and very cold; I was rapidly draining of all energy, my whole body started quivering violently. I shouted as loudly as I could at my scoutmaster over the noise of the motorbike engine and the traffic moving around us, with all the strength I could muster, I saw him look back and then down, and he instantly stopped the motorbike.

As he hastily dragged me off of it onto the road side, I couldn't tell what had happened, because the oversized helmet was blocking my view, and I began to feel sick.

Although I was unable to see the extent of my injuries I could promptly tell, from the now many faces stopping to assist, and from the lack of feeling in my left leg, that it really was not good.

As the wave of shock swept over me, I could feel myself drifting in and out of consciousness.

The look the scoutmaster had on his face, and the way in which he turned and looked at me, will be something that stays with me forever. It is an expression which I can see so vividly every time I re-live or recount this journey, whether talking about it, in my dreams or even now writing this. I see it always.

The look on his face was of absolute fear, and the memory of that exact moment in time is one which still jolts me awake some nights, and to this day still sends shivers over my spine.

Having been such a small child on the back of the motorbike, and not having the correct footwear on, (all I was wearing were trainers from the camping weekend which I had just attended), my foot was not able to accurately fully reach the rear passenger footrest of the motorbike.

Therefore the sudden nudge of the large pothole we had driven over, immediately caused the motorbike to jolt, which had in turn swung my left heel and foot straight into revolving rear back wheel of the speeding motorbike.

Still wearing the oversized helmet, and laying motionless on the grass verge on the side of the main road between Brighton and Eastbourne (The Main A27), in a time when mobile phones were very rare, one of the very first people to stop and help was a cyclist, he offered his assistance to my scout leader and rode off to the nearest house about half a mile away to get someone to call for an ambulance. To this day do not know who this gentleman was, but if for any reason at all he ever reads this book, and remembers his good deed, I thank you Sir, so much for what you did for me that day.

My scout leader straightaway tied a tourniquet around my left leg just below my left knee, he tightened it over and over in an attempt to try and help stop the vast amount of blood I was quickly losing, all of the time I could hear him telling me to keep talking to him, over and over he repeated it, "Marc talk to me"
I just wanted to rest my eyes, and relax but every time just as I was closing my eyes, again he would speak to me.

For me, lying there scared on the grass verge the time seemed to take ages for any help to arrive, although actually the ambulance did arrive fairly quickly, and the two amazingly composed paramedics took over my care from my scoutmaster.

Kneeling by my side they worked on me for quite some time, stemming the blood loss was their first major concern. Unaware of the full extent of my injuries I can just remember laying there on the grass verge virtually pain free, and relatively calm, looking up at the sky and seeing how the weather was getting worse!

My body began to relax, as the tension of anxiety about being on the motorbike was now over, it felt like the whole world was slowing down around me, in my limited peripheral vision.
I remember a police car siren getting closer and closer to our location and finally coming to rest somewhere behind the stopped motorbike. I couldn't actually see the car, just the reflection of the blue lights flashing onto to the reflective clothes of the people and objects gathered around me.

All of a sudden, without warning, people stated rushing around me with a look of horror on their faces, additional emergency services were arriving and I started to panic, I wanted my parents; I wanted familiar faces to tell me what was going on, I wanted them to hold me, and be around me.

One of the paramedics gave me an injection, and then started to give me gas and air through a plastic face mask, numbing any pain that may have been, and at the same time trying to help me to calm down. Suddenly I began violently shaking, I couldn't stop trying to move and get away from the situation; I wanted everything to be alright, and everyone to leave me alone.
Mumbling through the mask applied to my face, I kept shouting at the paramedic take me home.
"Let me go, let me go" I shouted as the odd tear slowly started to fall down my face. Every now and again I could feel the paramedics doing things to my foot, and still my scoutmaster looked on very concerned.

Finally and very slowly I was loaded into the ambulance, trussed up like a chicken to the stretcher, and with an inflated balloon boot on my foot helping to contain the blood loss. I was completely drained of any energy and it was then at this point that I remember instinctively feeling so ice cold, extremely scared and very alone.

Continuously drifting in and out of drowsiness, and full of shock, I heard the sirens blearing out from the ambulance siren as I was quickly rushed through the busy East Sussex traffic towards the Accident and Emergency Department in Brighton.

Strangely more than anything, I kept thinking, about how I knew the motorbike journey was going to have this kind of ending. The over play of this in my mind kept me constantly occupied until we finally reached the hospital, I was so disorientated when we arrived there that I didn't exactly know where I was, and this additionally added to my fear of being isolated and scared.

On arrival I was immediately taken out of the ambulance and rushed into an accident and emergency examination room followed by many doctors and nurses, all doing differing jobs. Some began by cutting off the remainder of my trainers and clothes; others were taking my blood pressure, and setting up drips, all of them running in and out of the room in a constant stream, through swinging doors, just like waiters going in and out of a busy kitchen.

My parents arrived a little later, once they had been found and informed by the police that I had been involved in an accident and that I was in hospital.
They had been out for the day with my brother and sister to the beach and were on their way home to await my home coming from my camping trip.
It was once I actually saw of my mother walking into the room that finally broke down in floods of tears, and only then that I actually began to feel the distinct pain that I was in. However somehow, now she was with me by my side I felt much safer, and not so alone.
Receiving one of the biggest and longest hugs in the world from my mother; I knew everything was going to be fine now that she was with me. Within minutes something was added to the drip and into my arm and finally I fell off to sleep.

What I didn't know at the time is that this was not going to be the only life changing thing that would happen to me whilst I was hospital.

My hospital treatment would continue for many months. Firstly at Brighton's Royal Alexander Children's Hospital, where all my initial operations were carried out by surgeon Mr Austin Brown, to stem blood loss which had been extensive, repair broken bones of which there were many (almost every bone in my left foot), and to fight off the many bouts of infection I had.

My time at this hospital was strange; initially for the first few days I quickly got used to being in hospital and actually started to enjoy the fact that I didn't have to go to school, and that I could lay around all day whilst the nurses brought me food. But as the time progressed and other children were recovering from their operations and being allowed to go home, I still stayed in hospital, and then time began to drag.

I had operation after operation. I never did enjoy having to be put to sleep for these, as it always scared and worried me that I may never wake up again.

Whether or not I would ever be able to use my foot again or in fact even if I would walk again was looking and sounding extremely doubtful, and because of that, the subject was hardly ever mentioned, especially in front of me.

The damage done had been so extensive that I don't think anyone really knew what the future held for me.

During the accident so much skin from my left heel was missing, that there was not enough left to even re-shape a heel from what remained, and a gaping hole was left.

During these preliminary months of sorting out the initial damage, reconstructive surgery was only something talked about as a very small possibility sometime "later on", and I didn't really understand what that meant.

Personally I was still unaware of the full extent of the damaged caused to my foot, as from day one it was continuously in bandages, or in plaster. In fact I never actually got to see the actual damage done to my foot until most of the repair was completed, which would end up being over 12 months later!

My mother, who was by my bedside always, every single day that I was hospitalised, did a fantastic job of being so positive in front of me always, she was constantly reassuring me that everything was going to be fine, even though it may take some time.

Her constant dedication to me whilst also having to look after my younger brother and sister, as well as keeping down her own job, was second to none, and is something which without question I am so very appreciative and thankful of.

I would never even know where to begin to try and repay her. She has taught me what love, caring and parenting really means.

In my life I can only aspire and hope that I am as good a parent to my children, as she has always been to me, my brother and my sister.

I now have the chance to officially thank her in print which means it will be documented for everyone to know, forever. X

I love you Mum so very much. Xx

Chapter Two – The Meetings

Life on the ward in the Children's Hospital, Brighton, became quite tedious, and the day to day routine of being in hospital became monotonous and very boring, suddenly I just wanted to go home and do the things I used to do, and spend some time with my brother and sister, and see all my friends.

I was able to watch some TV in hospital, but unlike today's more modern hospitals, with an individual television per person, this was in the time when portable televisions were wheeled around on trollies and plugged into the wall next to your bed.

Unfortunately however, there was only maybe one or two per ward, so not everyone got to watch TV. Some children were lucky enough to be allowed to go to the TV room, if they could move around freely, but I was bedridden, foot elevated in traction and constantly linked up to a drip. I always wondered what it looked like inside that TV room, everyone always came out of there smiling.

But I never went without; my mother constantly replenished me with games and books to occupy me, and the nurses in the hospital were brilliant and did all they could to keep me engaged and happy.

But at such a young age, I began to feel that things were not moving forward and I became very down and despondent. I just wanted to go home, and to be with my brother and sister and play and laugh and be back in my own bedroom.

Finally though, after almost two months of being in the children's hospital, discussions of possible reconstruction to my foot became more frequent between my mother and the doctors, although quite how and what was going to be done still remained unsure, and very uncertain, but the thought that progress was going to be made at some point soon filled me with a sense of gladness that shortly all this would be finally over.

The final decisions on my fate and my future would be left with the specialist skin graph and reconstruction team from Queen Victoria Hospital, in East Grinstead, and a meeting with them was requested by my surgeon Mr Austin- Brown, so once again I had no choice but to wait.

I recollect the morning two weeks later, whilst I was having my usual breakfast of two pieces of toast when my mother arrived to see me first thing in the morning as she always did. Almost immediately a nurse came over and asked to speak to her in private. When she arrived back at my bed side a few moments later, my mother was smiling and she told me that out of the blue, my appointment date had been brought forward through to see the specialist team, this was what we had been waiting for, hopefully now things could move forward a lot quicker and then soon I could go home.

We were going to visit these very "special" people in another part of the hospital a few days later, and they would review my case and hopefully they were going to give my mother a possible overview of any options that maybe available to me.
I was in a funny way quite excited, but also deep down a little scared.
I knew that these people would make important decisions about my future but I wondered what that would involve, and how rapidly they would then allow me to go home!
I was subconsciously thinking a couple more operations and I would be free to go home and restart my life precisely where I had left off.

All of the time whilst I was in hospital and especially when I was alone I would always continually wonder what my brother and sister were doing at home or at school, were they thinking about where I was?
Did they miss me as much as undoubtedly I did them?
What were they up to?
Were they happy and having fun?
When would they next come and visit?
Never did they ever leave my thoughts, especially after they had come and visited me. I never realised how much I would miss them, but as the oldest I wanted to be with them back at home arguing over minor things like all siblings do.

Finally, the "big" meeting day came along and all the waiting was over, my mother and I went to off to the crucial appointment, in another part of the hospital complex. We were both excited and slightly nervous as we waited patiently to see these very important surgeons. These people, in our minds were the people who could make such a difference in getting me finally better, and from what we had been told if anyone could do it, they could.

Eventually my name was called out by the lady on the reception, "Marc Richardson".

"This is it" my mother told me "here we go".

Entering the very large room, I began to wonder if these people were going to be able to help me at all, and if so what could they do for me? There were two gentlemen in the consulting room, one sitting behind large wooden desks in an extremely nice looking pin striped suit, and one in a long white coat who was standing up behind the other reading through my paperwork.

I can still remember the specialist's very first words to me, as he stood up from behind the large desk, he was very tall.

"Right young man" he said in a very stiff upper lip type of way, "What have you been up to then?"

The two men, a surgeon and his assistant took a good long look at the injuries to my foot, poking and prodding through the hole left in the heel of my latest plaster cast so they could see what was going on.

They then spent a while studying all the gathered evidence from Mr Austin Brown's notes, and all my X-rays, which had all been collated in a buff coloured thick folder on the old worn desk in front of them.

"I think we need to see if we can get you sorted out don't we mister, and quite soon" the Surgeon finally said.

The two men began to discuss things with my mother about what they may be able to do, and how they may be able to do it.

From the lengthy conversation they all had, all I managed to hear was. "Please be aware though this will be a long time process, and Marc will be admitted for quite a long period of time, and although we will do all we can, we still cannot guarantee anything at this stage"!

"Admitted for a long time" this kept repeating in my mind.

I just wanted to go home.

Almost immediately it was decided that literally within days, I was to be transferred from Brighton Children's Hospital to Queen Victoria Hospital, East Grinstead, Some 35+ miles away from where we lived in Brighton, (a 70+ Mile round trip for any potential visitors including my mother)!

I was going to be admitted onto "Peanut" Children's Ward, for what would turn out to be another seven and a half months of intense operations, and recuperation, including reconstruction and skin grafts, to try and rebuild the remaining parts of my left heel, and to cover the bones and the parts which were still exposed.

It would be during my time at this amazingly inspirational hospital, at the tender age of 13, when my whole outlook and perspective of life would absolutely change for evermore.

I later learnt that the Queen Victoria Hospital in East Grinstead, was built on its current site in the 1930's and developed as a specialist burns unit by Sir Archibald McIndoe during World War II, when it became world famous for the pioneering treatment of RAF and allied aircrew who were badly burned or crushed and who required reconstructive plastic surgery.

Most famously, it was where the "Guinea Pig Club" was formed in 1941, as a club which then became a support network for the aircrew and their family members.

Finally I had chance to leave the Children's hospital building in Brighton, admittedly it was only for the car journey to the East Grinstead hospital, but as I was wheeled out of the hospital in a wheelchair, at last I got to taste the fresh air of the outside world and I could feel the slight breeze on my cheeks again.

It was like an escaped convict, I felt free, and I just couldn't stop myself from looking around and taking in everything. The noises were loud and the people were rushing about, it reminded me that life still went on outside the walls of the children's hospital in which I had been "Held".

On arrival at The Queen Victoria Hospital, one a one hour drive from Brighton, my mother parked the car and we slowly found our way through the maze of corridors to Peanut Ward.

Everything seemed so different to the hospital I had just come from and I couldn't help but wonder about how long I would be in this hospital and when would I next experience the fresh air outside?

The ward was long, and each bed had its own private glass panelled cubical, and each also had a window, looking out onto part of the hospital gardens. It was much better than I had imaged it would be like.

The decoration on Peanut Ward was a marvellous mix of colour and amusing cartoon images, and at the end of the ward was a door labelled "Fun Room" which was completely full of soft furnishings for jumping around in, which unfortunately I was not allowed to go in, in case I injured or damaged my foot even more.

The room with it big red door was currently out of bounds for me.

One thing I noticed more than anything was the ambience of the ward, so many of the children were happy and smiling and seemed to really enjoy being on the ward.

Although all of this certainly made me feel a lot more contented, I still didn't want my Mum to leave me there, solely because I knew that I was now a long way from home.

"You will be fine ", she told me, "you will soon make friends, and I will be back every single day as I have done".

Of course my mother was right; I quickly met and made friends with many other kids on the ward and once again I quickly settled into the routine of ward life.

Being on the ward for such a long period of time, again I saw many children come in, have their operations and go again, each time this happened I wondered when my turn would come to leave.

Many of the children kept in contact once they left, and often letters or cards would arrive from them telling me what they were doing and wishing me better.

During the first month in East Grinstead I had a few initial small operations, some just to review the damage to my foot, others to regularly change plaster casts and dressings.

Some operations were to remove damaged skin and bone; others were to take small skin graft samples from differing parts of my body, such as my back and my thighs, some of which some were successful others were not.

As I learnt very quickly during this time, that skin grafts do not always work the first time, your own body can reject your own skin, and then the operations have to be repeated a few of weeks later.
However, very slowly and over a course of time, continuously bedridden and getting totally bored, things did start to improve, and the time was now right for the surgical team to start making the final changes to my foot, and an action plan was put in place to start one the many major operations which I had patiently waited so long for.

Steve was the hospital porter, who would always come and take us on the beds off to the theatre; he was a real fun guy and always made the kids smile, continuously whistling and joking. He would even whistle song requests, if he knew them, if not he would pretend to know them, whistling any old tune!

One day as normal Steve came to fetch me mid-morning.
I was off to the theatre for yet another operation, and this time the surgeons were going to remove a large piece of bone which had been left protruding from my heel, this bone had frequently become infected and now whilst they were able to, it needed to be removed before any kind of final closure of the wound could be done.

This operation was very important and needed to be done with so much accuracy, firstly the surgeons needed to identify how much bone could be taken away safely without too much blood loss, then they had to remove the bone and any damaged or dead skin around it, and hopefully they would be able to leave enough bone for me maybe put weight on in the future.

The final part of the operation would be a small, thin skin graph taken from my leg to cover the area in readiness for the main closure at a later time.

Many things including which type of final closure may be possible, and whether or not I would be able to walk on this foot again all depended on this operation and I was so scared and apprehensive, even more than normal.

Even though no one actually told me so, I could tell from the eyes of everyone who was around me that this operation was important.

This I hoped was the beginning of the end.

As we headed toward to anaesthesia room, Steve as always, told me jolly tales and funny stories and even sometimes deliberately pretended that we were going to leave the hospital in a fictitious planned breakout, rather than taking me to the theatre. Steve knew how much I really didn't like going to theatre and how scared I was, but his jovial comments always lightened the situation, and he put me at ease.

With every single operation I had, I always remember thinking how strange it was that one minute I was lying there looking up at the anaesthesiologist, and within what seemed like micro-seconds later, I was in the recovery ward being spoken to by the nurses and my mum. My first thoughts, after every operation was, I've made it through; followed by thoughts of how quick the time had gone.

On this day Steve eventually wheeled me into the anaesthetic room as he did every time, and after a few minutes of being settled and reassured I was once again slowly counting backwards from 10 as instructed by the anaesthetist..........10, 9, 8, 7; I could never seem to get past 6 before I was asleep?

But rather than immediately waking up in the recovery room almost instantly as I had always done, this time I immediately felt an overall feeling of love and warmth surround me. A feeling that still to this day I cannot completely explain, describe or depict in any appropriate words or expression.

It really felt like I was wrapped in love and heartfelt emotion, and nothing has ever come close to it since. Not even the extensive wide-ranging love I feel for my own children.

When I finally chose to open my eyes the view which was in front of me was not only breath-taking and remarkable but was also very disorientating.

Looking down from an advantage point somewhere up in the corner of a room from what seemed like a gallery, I saw a surgical team working away on young boy, I looked on absorbedly as they scurried around in the large room, and I felt overcome with many different emotions and I couldn't stop staring.

Suddenly I heard a soft but familiar voice calling to me from behind. "This way" the voice said "it's this way Marc".
I so was conscious of the ever increasing warmth and intense light behind me, calling me to turn and enter it, but I was literally transfixed, glued to the unfamiliar scene ahead of me.
I knew that soon I would have to turn around answer the person behind me, but at the moment I just couldn't.

The person with the soft tone spoke to me again, "I'm here for you Marc, we are all here, just walk towards me, and we can explain everything to you, please don't be scared."

With the overpowering feeling of affection growing thicker and faster around me I knew then that I now had no option but to turn around, especially when I heard further voices of characters which I distinctly recognised from somewhere.
"It's Ok" the voices repeated one after the other "everything is fine just come with us".
Finally I gave in and turned my head.

What I saw behind me I can only endeavour to describe to you, as I really do not know how to explain it appropriately enough with words.

Ahead of me was a brilliantly glowing, affectionately warm corridor which was full of "life" and philosophical emotions. Even though I could hear several voices, at the furthest end of this lit tunnel was a single elegant figure in dark silhouette, with an extraordinarily bright light behind it.

It was literally just there ahead of me, the end of the tunnel, as plain as anything I have ever seen.

"I can't come with you now", I answered, holding back from the now strong magnetism and pull of increasing light ahead of me.
I quickly turned my gaze back around to see the small boy still lying on the operating table.
It was then that I felt and heard someone approaching me from behind, and I knew that I would now have to go with them.

From over my right shoulder, I suddenly heard the voice of what I now know to be a cockney London male, and as clear as day it said into my right ear in a loud whisper, *"Look carefully mate, that's you down there"!*
I looked closer, what? How?
It was true, it was me lying on the operating table; I was watching my own operation. What? Why? How?
I began to feel like this dream really should end. I didn't like it anymore.

"Go back son" the man told me, *"Go back and I'll come wiv ya"*.

I couldn't take all this in as he continued, *"I'll be wiv ya whenever you need me, cos I'm taking back right now son, it all been agreed!"*

What do I do now? I distinctly remember feeling trapped how do I get out of this situation, my automatic reaction was to just close my eyes as tight as possible.

"Let's go now sonny it isn't ya time yet Marc..."

"Marc, Marc, it's all over now" I heard another familiar voice calling me "Can you hear me Marc, open your eyes"

Gradually I opened my eyes once more and letting them adjust to the light in the room, I recognised straight away the recovery room ceiling, but somehow this time it looked to be slightly brighter than normal and by my side as always was the recovery nurse. I felt relieved.

"Hello Mr", she said with her usual warm caring voice, "It's all over now your operation has been done, you just lay there quietly you brave boy and I will go and fetch your Mum she is so waiting to see you."
As I laid there slightly drowsy, I reflected for a moment on what I had just dreamt, Wow, that was odd!
That had never happened to me before, what a vivid dream, and I could remember everything and every single detail of my strange encounter during it. In fact I had never had a dream in like that in any one of my other previous operations.

My mother entered the room and came and sat with me for a while before we returned to the ward, and she explained that as far as she knew everything had gone well with the operation, but that it had been a fair few hours long, I could see the relief in her eyes.
The operation had been so long in fact that Steve had gone off duty that day, and it was not the same porter who was slowly wheeling me back to the ward this time.

I spent most of the rest of that day in and out of drowsiness, sleeping here and there and eventually trying odd bits of food and drink, and however much I tried not to, my mind kept instantly recalling all the things that I had so vividly seen and heard.

The following morning after a good night's sleep, and feeling much more awake I waited waiting for my Mum to turn up as usual.
A new ward nurse came over to me and asked me how I was, and enquired as to what I would like for breakfast.
 She was dressed in a peculiar uniform, greyer than the normal style, and seemed a little out of place on the ward.

Chatting away as usual, I asked her if I could have some toast, and I immediately began to tell her about my experience during my operation the previous day.

"That sounds interesting" she said, then quickly repeated my order to me and headed off towards the ward kitchen, obviously too busy or not wanting to continue the conversation.

A few minutes later my "favourite" nurse Lynn Edwards came over smiling as usual "Morning Mr What would you like for breakfast this bright sunny day, same as usual Toast?" ("Mr" was a name the nurses generically gave to all the boys on the ward, but it became more poignant one day when Lynn noted that Mr was also my initials.)

Lynn Edwards was a nurse, whom without; I would have undeniably gone crazy. Always smiling, however she actually felt, Lynn had time for all of us, and once you had heard the musical Welsh tone of her accent, you didn't want her to stop talking.
Sometimes she even brought me in treats which she had purchased or made at home. My day brightened up when I saw her.
I lost contact with her many years ago, but without her compassionate and thoughtful manner, my life at the Queen Victoria Hospital would have definitely dragged on. She truly was a children's nurse in each sense of the word and her radiant qualities and personality made her the Florence Nightingale of mine and many other children's lives on Peanut Ward.

I explained to Lynn that the new nurse had already taken my order for some toast. "We don't have any new nurses here today darling" she said, "It's just me, Sister Sue and Val here at the moment, have you been dozing off?"
I described the older nurse to Lyn in every detail, and with a quizzical look, she repeated that I must have been dozing off.
"I must have been", I said to her..... "I must have been.......I'll have toast please....."

Over the next few days after the operation, whilst I had to stay completely still in bed and rest, I tried on odd occasions to discuss my experience with my mother, and although she seemed to listen to every detail of what I was saying, I could tell she wasn't completely taking it in, or she was unsure that I had actually lived the experience.

But with her just nodding in the right places, and appearing interested was fine with me.

Besides, outside of driving the many miles every day to see me, she was also working a full time job, looking after my siblings and running the family home as well.

When I actually stopped and listened to myself trying to explain my experience to anyone who would listen, I began to realise how peculiar it must sound, and it was from that exact moment onwards that I decided to keep them to myself for now.

Besides I was on the mend, slowly, and as I had another operation due in a few of weeks, to place a skin graft which couldn't be completed during the last operation, maybe I'd have the same experience again and if not, I would know for sure that I must have dreamt it.

After a week or two I was eventually allowed to have some independence from my bed, which I had now been in for many months.

I was given an adapted wheelchair which had a plank of wood pointing outwards from the seat, to support my leg in the air, and on the seat was a thick pillow which covered one end of the plank which I had to sit on to keep it balanced.

Wheeling around in it made me feel like a tank with the turret sticking out, but I didn't care how I looked or how it felt, at least finally I could get around.

It felt to great being able to move around again and to have some freedom (even if it was only for the length of the ward).

For a change I went around visiting other children in the ward and played games (and some tricks) on them, rather than sitting in my bed having to wait for them to come to me.

As soon as I was awake in the mornings I couldn't wait to get into my "Transport", but my free time in it was limited by the staff nurse, as I did need to rest my foot as much as possible.

During the quiet moments of rest, or when I was in bed at night I did sporadically think about the "Cockney Voice", and sometimes I would hear what I thought to be some very isolated replies in my right ear, but they were not as clear as I had heard them before. Was this because I wanted to hear them?

The whole situation of what I had experienced was constantly on my mind and started to become frustrating, what was the explanation for it? Maybe the experience was something which came with having so many operations? Maybe everyone who had been in a similar situation felt the same?

Several days later along came the porter Steve smiling as usual, and he routinely wheeled me down the labyrinth of corridors.
Once again the nerves began to build and like all the previous times before, I became scared.
But as usual Steve made jokes about taking a trip out into the car park on the trolley instead of going to theatre. This time he said we could pop down to the local shops for an ice cream, however he didn't think I was dressed appropriately!
"The quicker you better" he said "the quicker you can go in the foam filled soft play room on the ward."
I really wanted to go in that room which I was prohibited from.

Eventually we arrived at the anaesthetic room and went in.
After a few minutes of reassurance from the staff and Steve, I was once again counting backwards from 10 as instructed.....10, 9, 8, 7...

"Marc, Marc, it's all over now" I heard the familiar voice.
"Can you hear me Marc, open your eyes"
Slowly opening my eyes letting them adjust to the light in the room, as usual, I recognised the recovery room ceiling, and the recovery nurse.

"It's all over now" she reassuringly reminded me.

This time there were no "other" voices or images, no "interruptions" to my operation just in and out as I had done many times before?
So the last time had to of been in my mind, a kind of dream, well at least now I knew for sure, but to be honest I was slightly disappointed.

Unfortunately the disappointment didn't stop there, a couple of days later my Mum and Doctors broke the news to me that the skin graft I had just had the operation for, had rejected and that it didn't take, in theory the operation did not work, and I would have to wait until a further operation could be done later in the month.

I couldn't believe it; my world was shattered, and now spending all this time being in hospital was finally getting to me. Now once and for all I just wanted to go home, and this time I meant it!

I began to rebel, I refused to do any work for the school tutor who came to the ward, and who I was meant to be doing lessons with me. Although she was a very nice lady, I just didn't have the drive in me to want to do anything for her, when I think about it now; I was actually very negative towards her.
I just felt deflated and I only had one thing on my mind, and that was getting out of this hospital and just going back to normal.
Like a typical stroppy teenager, I also began to stop eating and cooperating with the nursing staff.
"I want to go home" was all I would say, and I formulated a master plan.

Two days later when my mother went to leave she told me as usual that I needed to keep strong, and that she would be back again to see me the following day.
I broke down and sobbed and I told her "NO", I was coming home with her there and then, and that I was not staying another moment in hospital.
I grabbed the pair of crutches which I was that day given to try out, (as long as I did not put my bad foot on the floor), and I rushed in a very awkward way to get to the end of the ward before she did.

Once there I hooked one of the crutches through the handles of the ward doors, in theory locking us all into the ward, and now I think about it, stopping anyone from getting in! And I told my mother that I wasn't going to move the crutches until she would tell me that I could go home with her there and then "Right Now!"
Which of course, and quite rightly she wasn't going to let happen.

My roughly thought out, and shoddily executed plan including screaming my head off, lasted for all of about one minute, before it failed, badly.

My mother removed me from sitting in front of the ward doors, by literally lifting me up underneath my arms and she took me straight back to my bed, and placed me on it.
She abruptly handed my crutches to the nurses who had now come out of their office to see what the noise was all about, instructing them forcefully, not to let me have them back, or my chair, until I could conduct myself properly, and in a decent manner.
Then she kissed me goodbye on the forehead, and walked straight out of the ward.

That evening I felt so down, ashamed and alone, I sat in my bed sobbing for ages, why me?

Then I heard his voice again as clear as day, the cockney voice from the operation, *"dere's a lot more who's worse than you out there sunshine, you just wait and see"*, then he continued.

"I don't expect ya to understand any of this yet mate, but I am here for you and always will be, I will teach and show you everyfing I can about me and where I am, but not yet not me friend, not until the times right."

I was curled up on my bed, in a tight ball sobbing and I remember my only being focused on wanting to hear him again.
In my mind I repeated over and over "I will listen to you, but please talk to me again, who you are? What is your name?"
After two or three minutes of complete silence, the reply came, crystal clear in my right ear.
"Who I am mate, well that's a long one, we'll do that anovver time, but me name is "Tommy", and I am pleased to know ya fella. Keep your chin up cocker, and keep positive, and all always be 'ere!"

Tommy!

Now I had a name for the voice which I know this time I definitely heard, and Tommy was also right; there were people worse off than me out there.

Literally the following morning after telling me this, a young boy, was admitted to Peanut ward, in the bed right next to mine, and he had actually been blown up in an explosion and was completely covered burns in scars.

We became great friends, and seeing how he managed and handled his situation, really made me think about how lucky I actually was, and this helped me to cope so much better.

I trusted Tommy now and just as he suggested I spent the rest of my time in Queen Victoria hospital, being positive and committed to getting well and getting home.

I also did all I could to help the nurses and children on the ward, by doing odd jobs to help them out, from my chair.

Eventually, quicker than expected, the day came for what was ultimately planned to be my final major operation, although I knew I would have to have a couple more minor ones after this, hopefully I could now begin to get some closure to this part of my life, and I could then start the next steps whatever they may be.

This was still something no one could really completely answer, although possible "weight bearing" on my injured foot was now at least being mentioned by the doctors and nurses, as a possible next step "later down the line".

It was in the back of my mind, if during this operation Tommy would be there with me again, but more than anything I was totally predetermined on wanting this operation to be over and done with.

Following all of the other operations which had prepared my foot this final major operation would be one of the longest and most important operations I would ever have, the aim was to finally repair the hole left in my heel, the last piece in the puzzle.

The surgeon's plan for doing this repair was going to be by means of a Dorsal Flap type of skin graft.

In this operation the surgeons would remove the skin from the top of my left foot, (from the bottom of my toes to the bottom of my shin). They would leave this flap of skin connected to one of the main actuaries in my foot so it could survive with its own blood supply, and then they would finally turn this whole mass of skin and nerves around and position it to fill the final gap left in the back of my left heel, closing the wound and giving me a kind of reconstructed heel.

This was going to take the surgeons a long time to complete and several times during the morning they came around to my bedside to talk to my mother, and at the same time they drew all kinds of marks on my toes and upon the latest plaster cast, with different coloured marker pens.
If it worked this operation, all being well, really would be the beginning of the end, but what the end result would be, and after everything would be able to walk or use my foot ever again?

After a few minutes of the usual reassurance from the staff I was on my way to theatre. On this occasion Steve pretended to forget where we were going on the way to the theatre, and deliberately went the wrong way, leaving me to direct him back again.

Soon after I was once again counting backwards from 10 as instructed, but not for many more times I hoped.....10, 9, 8, 7 ...

Imagine if you can a very warm comfortable but bright room, however, everywhere you look in the room all you can see is bright white, the walls, floor and ceiling were completely white.

This is the situation I found myself in during this operation.

Then Tommy spoke to me, and whilst he did I could see slight shades of pale colours appearing all around me from every wall.
This was truly amazing and a situation which I will never, ever forget, I felt completely at ease, just like I was visiting a friend.

Within the colours emanating randomly on one wall to the right of me, I could see outlined faded images of the things which I were being told to me.

Tommy slowly explained to me that he was not actually living as I was, but he ensured me that I was not dreaming, and that he was very real.

He cautiously explained to me that he was a spirit, a special kind of spirit who was now going to guide me throughout the rest of my life if I wanted him to, and that this was something he had personally chosen to do, to enable me to continue my life here on this plain in a different way.
He told me that together we would continue these lessons regularly and that eventually over time I would be able to help others just as he was helping me now, but it would need a great amount of perseverance, dedication and time if I wanted to continue, and that this was entirely was my choice.
I didn't mind at all, as time was something that I knew I had plenty of.

"We will be a team now fella" he said *"Together as one"*

Those three words have been wedged in my mind ever since that incredible meeting and they mean so much to me, as they totally encapsulate the exact relationship I share with Tommy.
That is why I decided to have it in the title of this book!

When I woke from this operation, I can remember opening my eyes in the recovery room, seeing the nurse by my side and saying. "That's it isn't it, my new life starts here". I fell different, so very positive and more aware of the entire situation I had been in over the last 10+ months.

My mother came into the recovery room and I smiled at her. "I love you she said, it's all over"
A while later the surgical team came and spoke to my mother, they were very happy with how the operation had gone, although in their own words there had been "some complications and difficulties" but overall the 5+ hour operation had gone well.

Relaxation and bed rest for the next two weeks was now the prescribed treatment, and all we could do was hope that all the grafting was going to be successful and take hold.

I was positive that everything had gone exactly to plan.

Following a few more minor operations over the next two months, all of which Tommy was present at, the news was very encouraging.

The grafts had taken and were healing very well.
Everything had gone to plan; the doctors and surgeons were very pleased and amazed with my progress, and I could begin to see the light at the end of what had been a very long journey.

Finally all of my operations were now over, and I was really on the mend.
Surgeons and doctors were now also beginning to talk about my leaving day, under one condition, which was that my Mum agreed to be shown by them how to change my dressings regularly, (which she agreed to), and eventually a few weeks later the day came.

Although I was still unable to walk on put weight on my injured foot, now more than anything it was finally time to go home, even though months of extra physiotherapy, specialist appointments, and more home tutor work would need to be done, I was at long last departing the hospital and heading home, well over 12 months later than I had originally planned, and this time not on a motorbike either!

It felt exceptionally strange being able and "allowed" to finally leave Peanut Ward, which to me was not just a ward of a hospital, but a place which in reality had become my domain, my habitat for so many months of my life; it was also my protection and my security area, I had learnt and adapted to the routines of the ward back to front.

Lynn Edwards came in to work especially on her day off to say goodbye to me, she was the only person I kept in contact with until communication was broken a couple of years later.

I was never really able to tell her, but I would like to now take this opportunity to say; Lynn you are always in my thoughts ever since I left Peanut Ward and you made such a difference to my days in hospital and to me as a person. Thank you so very much. x

Just before leaving the ward for the final time the porter Steve came up to me and without saying anything he lifted me and my crutches into the air, everyone looked on amazed.

"What are you doing?" I said.

Still without a word Steve took me into the only room I had never been allowed, the soft play room at the end of the ward, and whilst securing my protected leg in his hand, he literally dropped me into the foam filled area.

"I told you and promised you mate that when your better I was going to make sure you went in here" he said, "now get out of here!"

With many hugs and kisses to a team of people who had not only nursed me back to health, but who had also become my adopted family, I left Peanut ward for the first and final time. Tears of both sadness and happiness filled not only my eyes that day.

Slowly clipping down the corridor, wobbling as I went, trying to get used to my new crutches with my bad foot elevated, we followed the signs towards the exit and out into the large car park.

It was again like tasting fresh air for the first time, and just as before the noises were loud, and everything was full of activity and seemed to be moving at such a fast pace.

Before long with aching red hands from the handles of the crutches we were in the car and leaving. I asked my mother to stop before pulling out of the car park so I could just briefly look back and remember the sight of the hospital.

"Don't worry" she reminded me "we can always come back and visit".

"I don't want to" I told her "I just want to remember it as it is now, so that the image will always be with me in my mind"

To this day I have never returned to Peanut Ward or the Queen Victoria Hospital, East Grinstead, but it certainly has a very special place in my heart.

Going home was fantastic, although it did take me some time to re-adjust back into "normal life" which was very different to the routine of the hospital.

I almost immediately learnt that by crawling around on my hands and knees and keeping my plastered leg off the floor that I could get around very quickly. This meant that that I could do things for myself and help out.

I found lots of time be an irritating eldest brother to my two younger siblings who I was so pleased to be with every hour of every day.
I really had missed them not being around me, so much so that it really hurt, but I never really knew how to tell them that.
We spent ages playing and laughing together and they loved taking turns using my crutches, which had became a new toy!

Nothing was going to stop me getting around and learning everything I could. I even did some of my home tutoring for my home tutor, although not always.
Since leaving hospital I became very positive in my life that nothing was going to stop me achieving my goals I was determined to get on, explore and make the best of my life, and every minute of it.

Outside of the house, I became an absolute master on my crutches, which I had now adapted, by cutting sponges in half and attaching them to the handles; it stopped me getting blisters on my palms, as I was always on them.
Sometimes I even amazed myself at how easy I could get about on one leg and crutches, and where I could get to.
On a family break to Somerset and Cornwall I even managed to venture through "Wookey Hole" on crutches unaided, and I also learnt that when I did need a rest I could hook my plastered leg up over the crutch handle to rest the weight of it.

Tommy was true to his word and was there with me, just as he had promised to be, and we would have regular "chats" together about the future, my future.
So guided by Tommy, and cared for by my wonderful mother, I began to make rapid progress.

One day whilst changing the dressings on my foot my mother asked if I finally wanted to see my foot, and what had been done to it? Up to this point I had not seen or wanted to see my foot or damaged heel.
My dressings were done with me laying on my front so I also never really had the chance to see it either, I decided that I needed to take look and see, my expression must of scared my mother as her first words were "it is much better now than when it first happened!"

I couldn't stop looking at what was now my "new" reconstructed foot.

It was covered in scars and wounds, and was a very different looking foot than I had imagined it would be, and it was at that point that it really hit me how lucky I really had been, and that made me cry.
I had never really understood the extent of the damage the accident had caused to my foot, and the reality and memory of it all came flooding back.

Looking at my foot I wondered what the future held for me and how this foot was going to affect me in my whole life ahead.

"Your just different mate" Tommy's voice said to me loud in my right ear, *"different is good, it makes you unique, and as we know you're not the same as everyone else"*

Chapter Three – The First Steps

A fair few months later, after returning home from one of my numerous hospital appointments with physiotherapists, doctors and specialists, I did what no one could have ever guessed or thought I would ever do again.

Although extremely wobbly, very unsteady and only lasting a few seconds, in front of my family I took my second step in well over a year and a half, on my injured left foot, un-assisted by crutches.

What a moment to remember that was. I think the smile on my face measured longer than the step I took, but wow it felt so good knowing I was making such great progress, no matter what anyone said or thought, I was utterly determined since leaving hospital to walk again on this injured foot, which had stopped me for far too long now.

The first step I took had been earlier on that same day when the specialist said to me, "All is going well young man, and you have made such good advancement, I think it is about time we got you to try and stand alone and walk a step".
Using the words of a famous astronaut you could say, it was one small step for me, but one giant step, toward the rest of my life.

Gradually, but as often as possible, I lessened the amount of time I needed the assistance of the crutches, and without doubt the strength and muscles began to grow in my left leg. Although very painful my foot was holding out with me starting to walk on it, and progressively as the weeks went by I started to weight bare on my injured foot more and more.
Because of the amount of damage done to my heel and the excruciating pain I felt each time I lowered my foot to the floor, I did however walk with a very prominent limp, which didn't bother me at all, because I was so contented about being able to walk around "normally" again.

However many other people seemed to be a lot more interested in the way I walked, as they used to stare and point at me as I slowly hobbled around my local area.

It didn't actually bother me, when I noticed them looking or staring at me, I used to deliberately wave back at them, or even walk towards them. They would soon then divert their eyes away.

There were occasional times when I would get upset about it, but just because I walked differently I was still a person with feelings.

I was very surprised at how some people did treat me differently; some shop keepers would even speak to me in a very slow condescending voice, just because I walked into their shop in a funny way, they seemed to think I must be mentally unwell or unable to understand them correctly.

Even members of the public would let shop doors shut in my face as I couldn't hobble quick enough to get to it before they let go!

In the beginning whilst I was trying to learn to walk again, and adapt back into "normal" life, having Tommy around me was great. I had so many questions I wanted to put to him.

"You have got a lot to learn my friend, it will take a long time, and there is an order to everything" he would always tell me.

But I wanted it to happen quickly, I was getting impatient and wanted to understand everything as soon as possible.

Being so keen to learn, Tommy suggested to me that I read books on certain subjects to keep my mind engaged and occupied. I therefore spent hours in my bedroom reading, especially books about life after death, and about people's individual accounts of their own out of body experiences.

Tommy was right again! I really could relate to these types of books, and I could understand the emotions which these people were explaining and trying to get across, and some of what I was reading was exactly as if I was reading about my own experiences.

Most of the descriptions and feelings completely matched those which I myself had experienced during my operations.

In fact I spent so much time in my room engrossed in reading that my mum allowed me to have my own kettle in there! It was my den, my haven, I loved my room! I loved having that time, reading and learning from Tommy.

Hour after hour when we communicated, I listened intently to everything he told me, trying as much as possible to understand and comprehend it all, it was a truly magical time.
Because nobody else could hear him, our "lessons" could continue on for hours into the night.

It would be during one of the toughest point in my rehabilitation that I finally began to realise how much I had a true friend in having Tommy around me, and that actually I should learn at his pace, as there was a reason why the "lessons" happened in a certain order.

Because I was walking with a very visible large limp, it was decided by my doctors that to counteract some of the limp, and to ensure I limited any further complications later in life with my hips, that it would be beneficial for me to have special surgically corrected shoes made.
So I went one day with my Mother to yet another appointment, this time to a new venue which we had not been to before.
We arrived at the specialist shop in Brighton, where a gentleman who dressed and spoke rather like he'd be more suited in a tailors shop in Saville Row, completely measured my foot was from every point, down to the nearest millimetre.
"These new shoes will be so much better for you" he kept saying over and over.
Even to this day I cannot tell you why, but I just couldn't connect with this man, something about him made me not like him.
I think it was just the way in which he spoke to me, his mannerism annoyed me and I found him patronising, and my mother could tell from my attitude that I was not impressed by him. Something she still remembers up to this day.

Several weeks later we were notified that the new shoes were now made and ready for collection. My mother took me back for the fitting and to collect them. I couldn't believe it when I saw the shoes.
When the gentleman finally produced them from their box, they were very old fashioned looking, shiny black and nothing like I had imagined they were going to be.

Each foot was so obviously and noticeably different from the other, where the alterations in size, length and width of my differing feet had been exactly catered for, they looked very odd indeed.

"These new shoes will be so much better for you" the man repeated again, exactly what he has told me the time before.

Trying them with a grimace on my face, they were certainly comfortable, and possibly would help me to walk slightly better in the long term. However the look of them was certainly not agreeable to the eye at all and to make things even worse the annoying man proudly announced that now this pair fitted correctly he could at this instant order a second pair to be put in production!

Usually I would not have worried at all about how aesthetically satisfying they were, if it wasn't for the fact that not only had I just found out that I would have to wear these shoes every time I walked from now on, and for some years, but that I had also just found out I was about to start a new school in two weeks' time.

I would be attending a new school in a brand new area, almost two school years after I had last sat in a classroom.

Children can be very cruel to each other, and on starting my new school, I was continually and repeatedly teased about my shoes, and about the way I walked for several months. Trying to explain to kids who did not want to listen as to why I had to wear the shoes was pointless, as far as they were concerned I was abnormal, different, odd and therefore a great target, for many of the children their sole intention was to upset me, and unfortunately it began to work.

To stop some of the teasing, and without the knowledge of my mother, I would swap my "special" shoes for my trainers which I had hid in my school bag, but wearing them all day, every day began to hurt me and made me walk even worse, which in turn enhanced the bullying.

On many occasions, after school, I would sit alone in my room and cry about how I was being treated by the other kids, and then I would become more upset, and I would often remember how happy I used to be prior to the accident.

Is this how it is always going to be from now I wondered?

During this very unpleasant and depressing time my only true friends were those who were interested in me as a person, and not just judging me for how I looked, and of course Tommy.

Whilst relaxing and reading in my room one evening after another difficult day at school from the bullies, I felt the warmth of Tommy coming close to me, as always approaching me from the right hand side. I asked him how I could end this horror I was having at school, I wanted it to end and I wanted it to end now, can't he do something?

A book which I had borrowed from the school library immediately fell from the desk in my bedroom straight onto the floor and landed with the pages open.

"Look at the passage in the book" Tommy said in my ear.

I looked at and read the pages which the book had fallen open at; the extract was about positive energy, and a small explanation about the differing types of energy which is around us.

After reading the pages Tommy very simply and serenely told me to just talk to those who were offending me, ask them what I had done to upset them, and how we could move forward.

"It's all about positive energy mate" he said *"show them your stronger in mind and in spirit than them, and give off positive energy against their negative energy"*.

I instantly thought to myself, that there was no way, me just having a conversation with these types kids was going to sort anything out, and besides, they were not the sort of people I could just ask to have a quite chat with.

I knew I had to believe in Tommy, if I was going to move forward, and this was something that would help me prove that he knew what was going on, and that he could actually help me with.

The following morning at school I kept thinking about what I was going to do, and what the repercussions could be if I got this wrong.

At lunchtime the main culprit of the bullying and his gang of followers started to walk over to ridicule me as usual.

What am I going to do now? I thought to myself.

"Just relax" Tommy's voice said *"I'm here with you"*

This had been the first time that I had heard Tommy clearly outside of my bedroom, now I felt so strong knowing I was not all alone, and that he was actually there with me too.

Extremely positively, but very calmly asked the bully straight out right, "Could you please explain to me why you don't like me, what have I ever done to you?"

Immediately his response was "because you're a cripple, you walk funny and look at your shoes!" he continued to insult me whilst roars of laughter came from his gathered posse.

Prompted by Tommy talking in my right ear, I asked him without delay, straight and with purpose if he actually knew how and why I had ended up in the shoes, and if he would like to know.

Under coercion from his own curiosity, and in case there was something else he could find out to taunt me with in the information I was offering up, he asked me how?

"You've got him now" Tommy said "Go for it."

Prompted by images and words given from Tommy, I explained my entire situation to him, every single gruesome aspect, all the blood, the gore and every pain, feeling and emotion which I had endured in my life over the last couple of years, ending with me hiding my shoes in my bag.

Slowly the laughter and ridicule eased off, and as I reached the end of my story all of the bullies' mouths were completely open and silent.

Miraculously by the end of that very same day we were all friends, and as word got around of my "new connection" with the schools "notorious leader", my bullying stopped almost instantaneously.

People started to be interested in what had happened to me, and wanted to find out if it was true what they had heard on the grapevine.

They also wanted to be my friend, and all were happy to help me at school, opening doors and carrying my bag if I needed them to.

I even stopped hiding my specially made shoes in by school bag once I had left the house in the morning and began to wear them for longer.

Tommy was right it was all about negative and positive energy, this was something I really needed to find out more about.

I learnt a valuable lesson that day. I must listen to what Tommy has to say always, and I must trust in him.
Tommy explained to me that he was always with me every day, but that I only heard him when I wanted to, the other times when I was preoccupied with my own things; I was not listening to what he may have been saying.
With our new understanding I could communicate and hear him whenever either of us wanted to, and wherever I was.

It was only then that I began to appreciate the things Tommy had to teach me, would take time to understand correctly, and that there was an accurate order to learning them.

"Now that you're finally ready to slow down and learn stuff in order, things are going to get interesting" Tommy told me.

Chapter Four – Lessons and learning

I was so excited that Tommy had decided it was time to step things up a gear with my tutoring, something which I had wanted right from the start.

The first and very important initial "lesson" Tommy taught me which I had to do every single day was to relax, and meditate, ensuring I had cleared my mind before "we" began to do any type of work together. I was lucky to now be living in the countryside and no longer dependant on crutches so I could take myself off to the local fields and just sit alone and relax after school by listening to the birds or the trees moving in the wind.
None of the "lessons" with Tommy would ever go right if I had a head full of things on my mind, such as any homework or revision that I needed to complete, nor would they work out if I wasn't in the right frame of mind to work with him, like when I just wanted to go out with my friends. If I attempted any lesson whilst not being in the correct frame of mind, I would just end up having to repeat the lesson over and over again.
I very quickly grasped how to relax and meditate each day, because I couldn't wait to start my subsequent lessons with Tommy.

The second lesson which Tommy decided should be next took absolutely ages for me to get right, but I never gave up.
In this lesson Tommy began to educate me on how to unlock my own psychic consciousness; he showed me how to use this capability to increase my responsiveness to his much faster vibration, and rapid way of functioning, something I had not realised until now.

In this lesson Tommy ask me to get a deck of normal standard playing cards, and by giving each of the individual cards in the deck, a basic image that I could relate to, Tommy showed me how to use these to understand what he was telling me.
For example; whenever I pulled from the pack the King of Hearts Tommy would say my name or show me an image of myself, so from then on I knew that if I saw that card physically, or received the image from Tommy in my mind, I knew he was telling me something about myself or something which related directly to me.

Once I had finally learnt all of the meanings to all of the cards, I would then sit looking at a randomly selected card; Tommy would give me up to five rapid images to process about that card and its possible overall defined significance.

I then had to confirm the image(s) back to Tommy that I believed he had given me for each card.

I loved this repetitive "lesson" as the cards were a visual way of connecting with people, and more importantly with Tommy.

Finally I learnt that whilst looking into the cards, Tommy could attach emotions and feelings onto me as well, now they all began to make more sense.

For example if Tommy showed me a King of Hearts and I felt a sad emotion, Tommy was telling me that I was going to be sad about something. It was like cracking a code or learning a new language, everything started to become so much clearer.

Tommy had obviously been communicating with me this way from the very beginning right back to when we first met, by using images as words, but because the pictures were being place in my mind so rapidly one after the other, I had not always seen or understood them. At the time I could not physically process the images he was giving me quick enough, and therefore I couldn't understand the messages he was giving me.

But by asking Tommy in the lessons to slowly overlay one image at a time, meant that I learnt to build a picture of what he was showing me, and eventually as the images got quicker and quicker, I could recall them in my mind.

Then Tommy didn't always have to talk; I just had to look deeper, feel the energy around me and watch the images.

Now finally I understood that the images and pictures were like another language, one which I had to learn and constantly keep on top of, so that I could work on the same higher vibration as Tommy was.

Today all of these years later I can now automatically and almost instantly tell what Tommy is telling me just by him showing me a random set of images, emotions or feelings, as most of them I have learnt or seen before.

If Tommy is telling me something new, such as a situation we have never come across before, and I do not recognise the images, I have to revert to working out each part of the message individually, the same as I used to do in the lessons, so I am still learning even up to today. It all seems so simple now but certainly didn't back then!

To me each new lesson that I completed felt like it was a small step forward and I couldn't wait for the next one.
The more lessons I had, the more I could feel how psychically aware I was becoming of the energies all around me.
I was now starting to walk into buildings and by allowing the images from Tommy to flow to me, and using all the techniques he had been taught, I could begin to feel the energy of the building or structure increasing.
I could hear soft distant voices connected with the location trying to tell me things, and I could repeatedly see past how the buildings looked now to how they may have looked or smelt back into their own past history.
This foresight which I had been given was remarkable and astonishing; Tommy truly had helped me to open up a true "gift", and every day brought brand new exciting insights, I now I certainly knew I was very lucky and certainly different.

One of the most memorable and emotional lessons we shared over the course of several weeks was when Tommy enlightened me about what happens when we pass from this life into the next.
He explained in depth to me that people who have passed over into the next life do want to reconnect with people here in the living, and that their reasons were not just to pass on communications and comments, but that for them being able to pass on these messages was also a learning curve in making them durable in the next life.

He gently explained how people's spirits or souls were not just gone forever once their existence on earth is extinguished.
This was an unbelievable and astonishing thing to have explained and shown to me, and was something I was so privileged to experience.

With this incredible insight I knew without a shadow of a doubt that I had so much more to learn, so much to comprehend, and so much more to do with my life.

61

Learning so much from Tommy, and having him around spurred me to want to study more and more, I became a total sponge for all spiritual information, I was reading as many books as I could about all different subject to try and enhance my own general knowledge and understanding of the "gift" that I and many others have.

With all this reading, learning and evaluation I was doing, I started to advance well at school, especially in subjects such as history, geography and art. My Mother and teachers noticed a vast improvement and progress in my school work, and all of my grades were getting better; I was even made a Senior Prefect at school as a reward for my complete turnaround in attitude and commitment to my education, which in all honesty had started a little unsteady.

Before long time had flown and my final exams came around and it was getting nearer the time for me to actually leave school, it was then and I learnt another very valuable lesson from Tommy.
I couldn't use my gift in any way to gain for my own benefit or advantage, nor could I use it to cheat!
I am certain that Tommy was there with me during all of my exams as he always was, but I never heard a peep from him, not an image not a word, or even a clue was given to me, (even when I asked for one)!

Having spent so long being engrossed in my own personal development with Tommy for so much time, meant that I didn't really spend much time thinking about the things maybe I should have, and I certainly did not have any ideas as to what I wanted to do as a career after leaving school, which was now quickly approaching.
My early childhood dream of wanting to join the Army, which really was the only ambition I had, was dashed the minute my foot was damaged in the accident, so I never really set myself a course to follow for the future, I had been much too busy with Tommy, and therefore I didn't know what I was going to do.

During one of my several part time jobs, just before the time of leaving school, I met a lady who was genuinely interested in my experiences and my gift.
I worked with her in a kitchen part-time, and we would spend many occasions whilst working, talking about Tommy, how it all came about and how I interacted with him.

She asked me several times if I would give her a personal reading.
She was fully aware that I had not actually done a definite one to one
reading with anyone, but she still insisted that she really wanted me
to have a go and do her a reading.
Eventually Tommy gave me confirmation that this would indeed be a
good idea, and a worthy starting point. So I arranged to do the reading
for her.
Being guided by Tommy, I asked her to choose a selection of playing
cards from the deck, (which I had been using during my lessons with
Tommy); so that I could enlighten her as to what they were telling me
about her.
Tommy would chip in with odd words here and there, and I recalled
the many images he had taught me about each card, as he passed
additional information to me.
The outcome was both unpredictable and astonishing; I was able to
connect to her life past and present and the information was coming
at me from all angles, and I even heard new voices pitching in with
Tommy's.
The lady was dumbfounded with her reading which she said was
"unbelievably accurate" she was actually moved to tears with some of
the information I gave her, and she proved the material was correct
by showing me photographs of the people and places which I had
been able to describe in full detail during the reading.
This was then the beginning of numerous other readings that followed
for many people who heard about what I was doing.
Even friends of my mother were now asking if I could give them a
reading.

I knew I wanted to do something with my life but was still so unsure
what that might actually be, so running out of time I decided, that as I
enjoyed working in the kitchens part time, I would to go off to college
and train to become a chef.

I trained at Eastbourne College of Arts and Technology, and although
had a great time, I knew in my heart that this wasn't the field of work I
really wanted to continue with for the rest of my life, my heart told
me so and I knew it. Standing and walking around all day was having a
really bad effect on my injured foot, the daily pain was becoming
unbearable.

After leaving college I spent a few weeks resting and trying to "find myself", where was I actually going in my life?

"What do you want to do", Tommy would ask

All I knew for sure is that I wanted to have fun and to have opportunities to meet lots of people, as connecting with people was something which I now fully understood, and talking to them recharged my own personal energy. I also knew from the readings I was now giving people that I was also making a difference to their lives as well, which made me very happy.

Following a lead from a friend, I made an off the cuff decision to join Butlins Holidays as a Redcoat and show compere.
After a brief interview with the entertainments manager, at the local Butlin's hotel, (The Ocean Hotel), Saltdean, I was immediately offered the position, which included all my accommodation and all my food thrown in as part of the package.
During my time at Butlins I got to meet so many people from all over the UK, including some celebrities, and I got to continue doing card readings for anyone who would let me, either during my break times or on my odd days off.
Without doubt I suffered quite a lot of pain with my foot in this job, due to the long hours I had to work, but the teamwork with my other Redcoat colleagues was so strong that if ever needed it they would always cover some of my duties to give me time to rest my foot for a couple of hours. In return I would do personal readings for them and their families when they would visit.

My lessons with Tommy had now moved on and were concentrating more on "energy". This included how to continue feeling energy around me from objects, other people, and the earth, and then showing me how to use it by giving it back out, to whoever needed it in a positive way. Such as friends who were feeling low or having issues at home.
"Energy Transfer" as Tommy called it was so exciting and by using it with positive thought, changes really could be made.

The seasons I worked for Butlins were without doubt, some the best times I ever had, and being given opportunities to perform in shows and interact with the large audiences was something I really enjoyed.

It wasn't necessarily that I was good at it, but more to the point, when I was on stage, I was able to feel the intensity of the energy flowing from the sheer number of people in the audience, and this gave my psychic awareness a major energy recharge.
With Tommy's help I was even starting to give development lessons to my acquaintances, showing them how they could better themselves.
I would also do a small meditation before performing and this would create a fantastic positive energy around us all, culminating in great shows and first class teamwork.

I really cannot move away from this section of my life without a mention to Mr Anthony Powers, my partner in crime on and off stage at the Butlins Ocean Hotel in Saltdean.
When I first started in the job Anthony (Tony) was instructed to show me the ropes, having been there for a whole season before me, he was well rehearsed in the way things ran at the hotel and very quickly he taught me the do's and don'ts .
Tony had an infectious personality and almost immediately that we met we hit it off. When we were on stage together warming up an audience before any major act or performance, we would "bounce" off each other so well that people used to think we had rehearsed our routines, well we never did, we just knew each other so well, every move or slight nod, meant something to each of us and our timing was impeccable.

Tony and I would form a friendship that would continue even up to today thanks to being reunited on a social network site. It is a friendship full of fun, laughter and joy.
Playing opposite him as my ugly sister in a Christmas pantomime one year was completely hilarious, and how either of us actually ever managed to complete that entire show I will never know. Along with the audience I have never personally laughed so much ever in my entire life, as I did that day, and boy did I need it.
Thanks Tony (my ugly "sister" forever).

Around the time I was considering leaving Butlins, I began doing more regular readings for people rather than spontaneous ones, as word was spreading locally of my accuracy, and I would often visit them at their homes; peoples attitude to mediums and psychic readings was slowly beginning to change, and more and more people were becoming interested in having these types of one to one readings done. Even so in those days readings were all still done mainly "behind closed doors" and were rarely advertised.

One evening following a request from a lady who had previously had readings from me, I tried to force too many readings into one evening at her home, and again I very quickly learnt a very valuable lesson about my very special gift, and about energy levels!
Trying to do too many readings all at once was not effective, it was rapidly draining my own energy and my ability to decipher all the messages which I was receiving from Tommy, gradually over the evening the images started to diminish and began mixing together, the readings were not going to well at all. I certainly learnt very quickly that evening whilst trying to untangle all the knots for everyone involved, that I have to treat this special gift with respect and look after it.
I also learnt that however much I try it is not always possible to get or give an answer to everyone all of the time, especially at the same time!
 "Lesson learnt" Tommy told me as we left late that night.

I found out through trying one day that I was unable to do a reading for myself, so after all of the experiences and constant lessons I had been having with Tommy, I decided that I wanted to find out how other people worked with the spirit realm and their guides.
I wondered if other psychics could tell me similar things to those which I was able to tell the people I was reading for.
How did other people use and work with their "gift"?

I began visiting local psychics and mediums near to where I lived, to see not only if they could enlighten me about my own life and where it was actually heading, but also to see if I could learn additional new techniques or ways of working from them.
Maybe at the same time I could also ask them how they became aware of their own ability, and how did they develop it?

Almost instantly and I found out that many of them couldn't actually tell me anything as specific or accurate, in fact almost all of them were giving me random answers and quotations which I couldn't actually say were related to me in anyway, and if they were they could have been mentioned just by probability alone.

Most of these people were just "cold reading" me, some of the information they were giving me was so broad and generic that it almost sounded scripted, and most of the readings came to an end dead on time, or to the exact second, that I had paid up front for!

I was very disappointed and dishearten, instead of gaining knowledge and the intelligence of new techniques, what I actually learnt was how I didn't want to work, and I had a very large realism check that not everyone who claims to have this magnificent gift uses it correctly, or to the best of their capability, if they have it at all?

I did however during this eye opening time receive from one lady (Joan), an amazingly clear reading; it was apparent that she was getting information from her guides about me, and she was very accurate about many things which had happened in my life including specific dates, and names connected to my accident and people I had met in hospital. She also noted my ability to work closely with spirit and energies.

However, at the end of the reading Joan told me I would marry a lady with the first initial of "M"?

At the time I was without question planning to marry someone with a completely different initial, and this really bugged me, as the rest of the reading had been so accurate and correct. How could she be wrong about such a definite thing which would take place very soon?

A few weeks later the relationship I was in ended quite quickly and the wedding was cancelled just days before it was due to take place. Around the same time, my end of season contract finished with Butlins, and rather than renewing it I decided with Tommy's guidance that it was time to *"get my own place"*, and get a *"proper job"*.

As always I learnt my lesson, and listening to him I started my new job a few weeks later, and it was at this job, that I would later meet the "M" of my life, "Mel". Xx

Chapter Five –
About me the person, my beliefs and my work.

To those of you who do have a true interest in who I am and what I do, let me try and give it my best shot at giving you an over view of me, Marc Richardson the person and my life, including what I believe in, based on what I have already learnt from my experiences and lessons from Tommy.

I will also endeavour to do my best to answer as many of the regular questions that I am asked as possible, hopefully covering those which are most interesting and that will appeal to you all.
Where do I start?
Good point.
"At the beginning!" Tommy says, I suppose he is right!

<u>About me.</u>

I was born on April 21st 1970, in Brighton on the South Coast of England, (making me a cusp baby Aries, Taurus), and I was brought up in and around the small East Sussex town of Lewes, famous for its large annual bonfire celebrations.
I have been so fortunate to of had so many roles models in my life including my two younger siblings, one brother and one sister, both of who mean the world to me, and who have always been there for me through thick and thin.
They both run successful businesses and they are the most wonderful Uncle and Aunt, to my two children, who admire them both.

My brother definitely has the "hands" of the family, being in the construction industry he can seemingly make or build anything from virtually nothing, and many times I have aspired to be more like him, but considering most of my construction or DIY attempts have later been rescued by him, I don't feel that there is now much chance of that!
Married and with two wonderful children of his own, who I adore, I am so proud of what he has achieved both commercially with his business and as a father. x

My sister is such a kind compassionate woman, who has worked so hard to get everything she owns, and whatever life has thrown at her she has come through it stronger and tougher, she really is a true inspiration to everyone who knows her, and I know she will continue to succeed in all she does with her business and her life. I am so proud of you. x Love you loads x

After leaving Butlins I started a new job, my first "real work".
I began working for an electrical retailer as a warehouse assistant and very quickly I worked up to being the manager.
This is where I met the "M" in my life, which I had been told about in the reading I had been given months early by "Joan".
I knew immediately, from the moment that I saw her that I wanted to be with Mel for the rest of my life, and Tommy agreed with me 100%. But how would she react to a limping, slightly overweight, new to the job, warehouse manager, who spent most of his time in the evenings either talking to himself or spending all night at other people's houses giving them readings from passed over relatives?

Mel has not only been my wife, but also my best friend for well over 19+ years, she really is my soul mate, and without question she is a wonderful devoted mother to our two children.
Her understanding and companionship in supporting me, with my work, and everything I do is so valuable, precious and immeasurable.

I think I would be right in saying that she has now got used to me not always listening or answering her when she is talking to me, as she knows that sometimes I am in "another place" with Tommy, listening to messages I am receiving, even if we are in the middle of a busy restaurant on holiday!
Sometimes though it is true to say that it is just "selective hearing!"

Mel, as well as running her own childcare business, looks after my diary and all my bookings. She arranges all my private events, which she often works on and attends with me whenever possible, and I really couldn't do what I do without her.
So again in print, here and now I would like to say:
Thank you my darling for everything you do, I love you more than you could ever imagine and more words could ever express. x
Always and Forever, Together x

Now that our two children a son Luke and a daughter Lauren are growing up, both in their teens, they are becoming more interested in my work as a Psychic Medium, and both of them are asking me more and more questions about Tommy, and how I got to be like I am.
I hope they will read this book one day and learn something from it, and even if they are the only ones to ever read it, it would have achieved one goal.

I love you both with all my heart; you are my worldly possessions and you mean absolutely everything to me. Please know that I am so very proud of you both, and everything which you have achieved so far in your lives. X

As I sit here now, proudly typing away on my first book looking back throughout my life so far, recalling many old memories, I am indeed very lucky to of have so many role models playing so many parts in my life, and I have certainly learnt something different from all of them.

I honestly would not change a single thing which has happened to me throughout my life, from the amazingly good times such as when my children were born, to the heartbreakingly bad times including my accident, because everything which has happened to me, has made me the person which I am very happy being today.

Whatever their personal beliefs, my entire family supports me in my beliefs, and they understand and know how much it really means to me, and this support is so very important, as it helps me to continue doing what I do. Without it I would not have been able to achieve many of the things which I have, including being nominated for a spiritual award in 2009/10, something I am so very proud of.

From the very beginning just after my accident, my family became used to every now and again finding me chatting away to myself, and they even started telling others about my "imaginary friend", which they wrongly but very comically nicknamed "John".

They used to say "is that John again you're talking to again"
"Does your friend John want dinner tonight too?"
"Is John coming with us?"

Even years later, on our wedding day, the whole family who were now fully aware of my "imaginary friend", had an empty place set at the top table for "Tommy" to sit at, and believe me, he was there alright.

I have during my work so far, had the privilege of working alongside some of the UK's top Psychics and mediums on several events, including TV medium and exorcist Mr Ian Lawman, Ian is not only a fantastic guy, but he is someone I am privileged to be able to call a friend.

For 15+ years I have, along with all my spiritual work, ran and overseen my own logistics company, which gives me something different to work on and look after, and it keeps the mind active.
I also decided to get more involved in Mel's childcare business, being that she does everything for me, and I was very proud of myself when I completed an NVQ3 in Childcare, and more recently my NVQ4 in child care learning and development, so that if ever need to I can help her out in return.

I certainly try as much as possible to keep as active as possible within my local community; I arrange many events to raise money for local charities.
One such annual event sponsored by my company has been "Who Has Talent", a platform where local people of all ages could apply to show off their own unique talents to the rest of the community.
For several years this show culminated in a "Grand Final" at the prestigious Theatre Royal in Brighton, in front of an audience of around 1000 people, and was hosted by myself.

All proceeds from all the shows went to chosen charities including The Anthony Nolan Trust, a pioneering charity that saves the lives of people with blood cancer who need a blood stem cell, or bone marrow transplant, and more recently Albion in the Community, the charity arm of Brighton and Hove Albion Football Club.

Also every year my company also sponsors "Let's Dance" at the Dome in Brighton, a show in which hundreds of children from many schools in the local area of Sussex, of all ages get the chance to showpiece the dances they have worked on.

As a family we attend every year as VIP guests and there is nothing more rewarding than watching these youngsters showing you what individual talents they have, whatever their age, size, colour or ability. Watching them smile makes me smile, it reminds me of the days I was on stage at Butlins, and I am proud to be a continuing sponsor.

When I am working with people either when I am doing readings, events or development courses I am often asked so many questions by the wonderful individuals I meet about my gift and my beliefs; these include questions such as;

What do I believe actually does happen when we die?
How do I use my gift on a day to day basis?
Have I seen a ghost?
What happens during a reading?
Can you tell me the lottery numbers?

Most of the questions, I am asked are from inquisitive, honest and very open minded people who are genuinely interested, in what my beliefs and opinions are, and almost all are actually interested in finding out more information, not only to satisfy their own need to understand my gift further, but also because they don't necessarily know any other psychic medium, and they have a thirst to gain further knowledge or another perspective on what they may believe or have witnessed themselves.

However I have been asked, and do still get asked questions from some people who are only trying to ascertain if there are "holes" in my "theory" or in the consistency of what I am saying.
I have never had any problems on any occasion in answering any question about my gift or my belief to anyone, as I know from what I am told, and from what I have learnt from Tommy that the answers are correct, and completely consistent.
I also fully appreciate that my view, is just that, and I would never and have never, forced my belief on anyone, and nor do I believe that any true honest psychic medium should or would.

To all those people reading this book, who may be sceptical, and wish to prove that the things I say are non-meaningful, false or fabricated, I completely value that you have an opinion and I completely and totally respect that this is your interpretation, and you are very much entitled to it.

Therefore I can only but ask two things of you. Firstly that before you dismiss anything that I or any other medium or sensitive has to say, please at least allow them the respect to authenticate themselves to you to the best of their ability, and secondly, why are you actually reading this book?

So what are my actual general beliefs?

First and foremost, above anything else, I do honestly and truly believe that my role as a psychic medium is to give evidence to and assist those who may need my help.

Wherever, and whenever possible I should do all I can to try explain what I know, what I have learnt and have been taught, to as many of those people who are interested as possible, as well as assisting them to develop their own abilities, in linking with whatever is around them, including spirits and energy in general, if they so wish.

So that then they too can better their own understanding of what is actually happening around them.

I myself do not follow any particular religious belief or faith, although I have done research into, and studied, many of the different religions.

I find them all extremely interesting, especially as there are similarities between some of them, and I totally respect that everyone has their own views and beliefs on this subject.

Whatever anyone's beliefs are, they should be completely respected and they should be allowed, without prejudice, to follow those beliefs.

Personally I follow my own path, and that is a spiritual path, which I am shown and guided through by my spirit guide Tommy, every step of the way.

Each new day for me is another day of learning and another day of living my life to the fullest. Important in that belief, is having my family and friends around me whenever possible, or at least being in regular contact with them.

I get so much personal satisfaction from being around those I care about, ensuring that every moment we share are good ones. I would rather here laughter and happiness than conflict and arguments.

Those people, who know me well enough, know that I am thoroughly dedicated and always inspired to continue doing what I do.
I openly admit that this devotion is not always straightforward, it can be very exhausting and remarkably draining at times, as well as being particularly emotional, and it certainly requires me to devote vast amounts of my time, listening, reflecting, meditating and sharing.

It goes without saying that I do believe unequivocally that there is another existence after this one, that we are all currently living now.
I have personally heard, felt, seen and been shown far too many things throughout my life as a psychic medium to think or trust anything differently from that belief.
I know that when we pass from this life, our spirit moves on into other dimensions, ones that we are not all truly fully able or ready to comprehend currently, and even ones that even I am still learning from Tommy all these years on.

However I do know from my own experiences as well as what I have been taught, that the next world is full of love and understanding.
It is a place that we all go to, it has no psychical time but is full of education; true contentment, remembrance and caring.
I know that when our time comes we will all be guided through it and shown how make a difference to others if we so desire.
It is a place where so many choices, mean there are so many future options ahead of us, and all of this happens after our life here has ended.

I believe that when we pass on from this world our spirit will remain close to those we love and are around now, and I also know that we will be there for them, to meet them, when they too pass over.

I also completely believe that we are all responsible for our actions whist fulfilling our lives here and now, (Karma), and that we will keep returning to this life plain in differing forms over and over until we do learn to live our life correctly and to its fullest, making the most of every opportunity.

75

This includes treating people the way we would like to be treated, helping others in need, and not just crossing the road to avoid giving help to someone, speaking to people as people and not as things, connecting with the earth, the trees and the planet which we live on, and being positive towards each other.
All of these things cost nothing, but can make a complete change to the way we all live, not only as individuals but together.

Our spirit in the next life is free and able to move around, and whilst doing so we are learning things from others all around us, including those who have passed before us. It doesn't matter what your belief is now, we are all given the chance to progress when we pass over.
I accept as truth from Tommy, that all of those who may have done "wrong" in their lives will have to at some point re-live and compensate for what they have done, by making a positive and constructive difference, to human life before they themselves can finally be accepted to move forward in any spiritual realm should they wish to do so.

Those close to me, also know that I am a without a doubt true believer in "what goes around, comes around" and I also believe that "everything happens for a reason".
Why we meet certain people at certain times in our lives and what that can lead to is all for a reason, and consequently we should treat everyone we meet with respect, as very often your paths in life will certainly cross again sometime in the future, even if you think it is unlikely.
You never know when someone you have previously met could be the person you need one day, and they may even end up being the person who can make a decision which will change your life!

I know that one day everything I have said or ever explained to people, will be able to be proved by advancing science and that as time goes on more and more mediums and psychics will be taken more seriously, this is a time which personally I cannot wait for because I believe "real" mediums could make a "real" difference to the world as we know it.

Just as I think that those who are not truly "gifted" will be exposed and that then ultimately, many more people will then be able to move forward spiritually in a more truthful open way with each other.

I know that I am incredibly fortunate and privileged to have so many people; both regular and new, who want to have personal readings with me, and I thoroughly enjoy this part of my work.
People contact Mel continuously through my website or on the telephone, and she does everything possible to book as many people in as she can for readings with me. She then instructs me on where to go and who to see next.
However more and more often, there are unfortunately far too many people wanting personal readings for the times that I currently have available.

So when Mel was asked one day by someone who had come and had a reading with me, if I would be able to go and do an evening of clairvoyance for over 100+ people, who all wanted to see and hear me work, I jumped at the chance.
I have to admit I was at first very nervous, because I did not want to over work Tommy or myself and end up with a room of people, all getting mixed up messages, I had learnt this major lesson from the early days!
However, Tommy gave me the thumbs up sign, his "clearance" to go ahead. I knew that this way I could get to see more people at the same time, and that then I may be able to give a few more people a message.

So the evening was booked and planned to go ahead.
I arrived at the venue with Mel and a couple of people who set up some sound equipment. Before long the place began to fill up.
The whole audience was very warm and welcoming towards me and the evening was a great success.
Tommy worked very hard to assist me in handing out numerous messages to the many that had turned out. Including; one lady who got a birthday message for her husband, from his father who was in the spirit world, waiting to say "Happy Birthday and I love you!" and he reinforced this by giving out his nickname for his son, which only a few people ever knew of.

Another lady was reunited with her best friend who was in spirit, and who had always said she would return one day and give her a certain message, well she did, as well as giving out some very funny details about her friend's eating habits!

Even apparent sceptics in the audience managed to get messages, which left them scratching their heads and coming up to me after the event to say thank you, and how do you do it?

However many people it is for from 10 – 500, I love these types of evenings with groups of people, because it initiates conversation about things they probably wouldn't normally discuss.

Looking at the faces of people smiling as they leave, talking to each other gives me so much pleasure, and being able to tell someone that their brother misses them, and that they are fine, as well as to pass on such intimate details is incredible and very emotional.

I can see from the faces of the audience as they vacate a venue that they leave more positive and that for me is what my gift is all about.

One thing I do not think people understand, is how hard it can be giving out readings, especially when you know the minute you say a few cherished words, you are going to change that persons views of the world completely. When it happens, which admittedly is not every single time, it is absolutely amazing, and often I finish readings totally exhausted, from being the linking piece in a conversation between the two worlds, and at the end of the day is it really worth it?

Most definitely!

Another important part of my work, I believe is to help others to develop their own psychic awareness, and to find their own inner self.

I hold regular development evenings and courses to allow people the chance to advance and understand what is going on around them personally. I always try to get the whole group working in total positive synchronicity with each other's energy, and I am sure those who have attended will tell you of the amazing results we have had.

I believe and know for certain, that I cannot use the gift which has been given to me to benefit or to enhance my own life financially and nor can I use it for anything other than its purpose.

So unfortunately I cannot predict the lottery numbers for this week either, but if I had one pound from everyone who has asked me that question, I would be very rich!

Giving personal readings.

When someone books with Mel to have a personal reading with me, excluding those who may come on a regular basis, I do know anything about the person in advance. (Except sometimes Tommy may offer the odd word or image prior to me actually meeting the person).
On occasions I visit people at their homes, but more often than not they come to me for their reading. On arrival I show the person to my "reading room", which very much like the rest of my home, is designed to be comfortable and welcoming. It is an area I have specifically chosen and which has been decorated by me, (guided by Tommy!) in which I relax ready to start my readings. I much prefer to do the readings at home not only because I can relax easier, but it also rules out any possibility for the person having the reading that I could be cold reading information from items in their home, such as pictures.

I always explain first and foremost than I cannot, and will not guarantee that any spiritual connection will take place.
Until the person is actually sitting in front of me and the reading begins, I do not know if any spirits will come forward for them.
It has happened on occasions, when I have not been able to get a spiritual message for the person having the reading, even though Tommy is with me all of the time, ready to pass on any messages.

I understand that for the person having the reading this can be extremely frustrating, but there could be many reasons for this.
Including the fact that the spirit energy does not think the receiver is actually ready to hear the information they have to give.
Any message which emanates from the spirits comes as and when they want it to and these messages will not always be the messages which the person having the reading is expecting to get.

I specifically remember doing a reading for a young gentleman one afternoon who very strongly told me that he would know for certain if it was his mother who was communicating, just from the things she said and the words she used.

During the reading he did certainly confirm that the messages I gave could only have come from his mother. However he really wasn't expecting the meaningful "telling off" that he got from her for not looking after himself, or the special Roses which his mother has nurtured for many years!

To ensure I am able to offer those coming to me for a reading some kind of information, I do not just rely on messages from spirits. Thanks to Tommy and the way in which he has taught me, I can also use playing cards and my clairsentience and other abilities, to give the person some kind of a reading even if I am not able to make any spiritual connections.

Without trying to seem rude, I always try not to have too much eye contact with the person during the reading, as again I do not what them to think that I am "cold" reading them from their body language.

At the end of the reading I always allow everyone time to ask me any questions which they may have, which I will answer to the best of my ability along with help from Tommy.

All I ask of any person who comes to me for a reading is that they are, open minded, respectful, positive and honest.

Booking a personal reading with me can be done via my website: www.marcrichardson.co.uk

Working with the Paranormal.

We can never learn too much. I am always interested in learning more, about what my gift has to offer, so as part of my work, I am also lucky to be involved in Paranormal Investigations.

Many people wonder why I do work with the paranormal, which is a really good question, and there are a couple of reasons why I decided to do this as part of my work.

The first reason I am interest in being involved in these events, is that as a psychic medium, and someone who loves energy from everything around me, including historic buildings, I have been able and extremely lucky to have visited, worked in, and investigated some of the UK's most magnificent locations, and normally when they are quiet or empty of the general public.

So personally it is a great chance to spend some quality time in these types of venues alone, learning from Tommy and honing my gift. What more could I ask for?

My second reason for attending these paranormal events and in some ways more importantly, is because I wanted to make sure that they were being done correctly and respectfully to spirits, and that they were not just a "ghost hunt".

It is true that some spirits can become "trapped" or "fixed" to a location, that they do not want to leave, and that they can remain there indefinitely, happy in their own way and this is their choice. Others require help to move on, but all spirits whatever their circumstances need to be respected and dealt with accordingly and appropriately.

When I work with the paranormal it is done with the greatest respect for the spirits, as I know from Tommy that many of these spirits are just re-living their lives over and are happy doing so.

Unfortunately though there are some companies out there just running these events as a "Ghost Hunt" and some, not all, go to great lengths to ensure you get a "frightening" experience.

In my opinion these companies have jumped on the mass curiosity people have shown, on the back of television shows, and they are only out there to hold out their hands and acquire vast amounts of money available from people who are genuinely interested in understanding the paranormal.

Some of these companies do not even get experienced people to run their events, they use people who do not know anything about what they are supposed to, nor do they have the skills to carry out such events.

Some companies even do all they can to call in or antagonise spirits, in the hope of physical evidence happening in front of their clients, and if nothing happens they make it up or hoax evidence.

On a few odd impulsive occasions Mel and I, as well as a good friend Lucy, have paid for tickets and attended random evening or overnight paranormal events, just as a customer, to see what some of these companies are actually doing and offering to their clientele, and for me it really can be a shocking experience.
These type of badly organised events remind me of the times when I was receiving false readings from people myself, charlatans who are trying to make a quick fortune.

On one specific occasion which comes to mind immediately, we attended an event run by a large company. We paid £55 each as well as the other 35+ guests and we were literally left roaming around a venue on our own for more than two hours, with no instruction or assistance from anyone.
We would have left the event and gone home for sure, had another one of the paying customers not recognised me from my website, and without question began telling everyone that I could take them on a vigil of the venue, which obviously I did, much to the disgust of the event organiser, who then eventually gained some interest!

I am constantly being offered numerous opportunities to join paranormal groups from all over the UK, and I have turned many down.
I do obviously have my favourites who I have worked with, because these groups have worked hard on allowing the paranormal experience to be a "real" one.

The staff members working on these events, and their professionalism has made the events run well, and I enjoy the respectful way in which these certain companies work.
More importantly all of these companies allow time for questioning and discussions before, during and after their events, which is what is certainly needed, especially for people who may not have ever attended an event before so that they have time to have time to understand everything correctly.

It was on one of these well-established events that I met Hazel Ford, who gave me many opportunities to meet lots of people, and to share my knowledge with them. For a while I worked on many of her events across the UK, including a promotional event for Paramount Films in London.
Thank you Hazel x

In turn for working in the paranormal field, I have been able to spread the word of my gift to so many wonderful people both believers and sceptics alike, and these events have also given me the chance to meet and make so many friends including but not limited to the following people;

Christine Miller
Gary Smith
Jayne Hendy
Jenny Semmence
Karmen Waldron
Maria Clare-Lush
Martin Gregory
Sharon Wilson
Stuart Cox

Whilst continually working on paranormal events, for several months I was very lucky, to be driven from location to location by another amazing guy who I am so privileged to know, and who has become a great friend of mine.
Obviously I can only be talking about Mr Kevin "Drebin" Ling, as I have nicknamed him.
I have spent so many hours in Kevin Ling's car; travelling so many miles across the UK that I wouldn't even want to start adding them up.

With "Muse" banging out from the car stereo, mile after mile, hour after hour, "Kevo" as I affectionately call him would drive me from one location to the next.
During the time I spent with Kevo "on the road", we shared so many entertaining moments that sometimes I really couldn't breathe from laughing.

Kevo always got us to a place, eventually, (even if we sometimes had to get the locals to guide us), but on arrival having to deal with the parking, well that's a completely different story, hence the nickname "Drebin"!

Kev if you ever do read this book mate please know this from the bottom of my heart, you are a star, a first class acquaintance, a wonderful guy with a heart of gold, and your someone I am very blessed and fortunate to be able to call my friend. Thank you so much for everything x

One of my absolute favourite paranormal investigation groups is without a doubt, Tricorn Paranormal, run by Mark and Sue, who I first met when they were working for another Paranormal Group.

Tricorn Paranormal, in my mind, stand for what paranormal investigations and experiences should be about.
Mark and Sue are dedicated to ensuring all of their clients are happy, and enjoying their evening. It is the experience of attending these events that they offer to people, and not a fixed, already planned package like some other groups. Although Mark and Sue always explain to their clients, that nothing on their events is ever guaranteed to happen, I can honestly say that whilst working on their events, I cannot think of one evening in which something amazing has not happened.
A lot of this I believe is due to the relaxed, respectful and very professional way in which they run their events.

Mark and Sue have asked me on several occasions to come along on their events as a guest, and I always jump at the chance whenever possible.
Together with them, Mel and I, (and of course Tommy) have investigated many differing UK locations, and annually as a team we investigate unusual and interesting European places.
Over the last two years we have investigated the Somme region of France, each time with fabulous results including; audible voices calling to us, voices answering questions when clearly no one is around, and even a mini bus shaking and its battery being drained almost on cue.

Tommy loves working on their events because of the positive energy they create, which in turn helps people to learn.

On occasions Tommy has even given Mark and Sue silly fun nick names into my ear, and obviously as Tommy has told me, I have felt it essential to tell them what they were!

Mark and Sue both have Psychic abilities, and on occasion have come up with some very accurate information. This has led them both into wanting to know and understand further what is happening with their own personal development, and I hope that I have been able to guide them on that path.

Mark and Sue are great friends and a wonderful couple; we have all shared not only some remarkable and inspirational phenomena, but also so amazing times full of fun and laughter.

I was totally honoured when Mark asked me to be his best man earlier this year.

Thank you to you both for your continuing support, and both Mel and I look forward to many more wonderful times ahead in the future. X

One thing is consistent throughout all my work, and that is the questions people ask me. I never mind answering any questions so to finish this chapter I have answered some of the other most regular questions which I get asked on or during events.

What is your favourite Haunted UK Location?

This one is very hard to answer as every location I have been to offers a different experience and has differing energies connected to it.

I love them all is the honest answer.

But if I had to pick, one of my most favourites is the place I feel most connected with, which is Michelham Priory, in East Sussex. This is a very beautiful historic property nestling deep in the Sussex countryside and it offers a great energy lifting experience at any time, and is well worth a visit.

Have you ever seen a full apparition?
Yes I have seen several full apparitions throughout my career. The first full apparition I saw was of a young man, who in a lesson with Tommy one evening in a church graveyard, showed me by pointing to where he was buried.
Since then I have seen several more whilst in a collective group of people during paranormal investigations, as there is more energy for the spirit to acquire and make use of.
However I have to point out, seeing an apparition is indeed generally a very rare occurrence, so I have been very fortunate.

What is the scariest thing you have ever seen?
To be absolutely honest nothing I have seen has really ever scared me, as Tommy is always telling me what to expect and how to control the situations I am in. But I have been, on several occasions, in situations where I have felt slightly out of control. One such occasion I was in house where in front of six people the words "Get out now" were slowly appearing in hand writing on the wall in front of us.

On a recent investigation in France I saw myself in "my mind's eye" being lined up in the sight of a rifle, seconds before everyone who I was explaining this to in a group heard a rifle being cocked!

But nothing really, actually scares me, apart from my kid's mobile phone bills!

Have you ever been hurt during an investigation?
I have had many objects thrown in my direction when working on investigations, such as stones and screws, but none of them have ever really hurt me.
These things happen by spirits who are trying to grab my attention. There was once, on location in the UK, and on video, when my arm was without warning pulled into a room and seconds later it was removed covered with small bleeding scratches, but again this never actually hurt.
It was however very much unexpected!

What keeps your energy going during a paranormal investigation?
The most important thing for me during any investigation is to keep
my own energy high, so feeling the positive energy from the people I
am working with is imperative.
If everybody is working together in psychic synchronicity my energy
will remain high.
Also I am without question addicted to coffee from a certain coffee
retailer (the one with a green logo), and I am partial to the odd energy
drink and a Milky Bar or two.
Having Mel with me on an event whenever possible is also great and
very important for me too, as she has a natural capability of just
looking at me and knowing what I need to top my energy levels up,
even if that's just a quiet word or a hug.

Can pets hear spirits?
Yes for sure, animals and young children are very open and receptive
to spirit and psychic energy. Which is why many animals suddenly look
up when there appears to be nothing there, and why some children
have regular long lasting imaginary friends.

*Have you ever heard from one of your own relatives who have passed
over?*
I sometimes get snippet "updates" from Tommy about my own
relatives, but I never actually have chats with them.
I know that they will be there when I pass over, so I look forward to
seeing and chatting to them then. However I did on one occasion get a
telling off, from the other side, from Mel's Nan whilst on location,
which came as a bit of a surprise!

How do you relax, switch off and recharge?
I never really switch off, and I do suffer from insomnia, so several
nights a week I just cannot sleep or switch my brain off, however
taking a good long walk along the beach certainly helps, and spending
good quality time with my wife and my two children certainly relaxes
and recharges me. I love the theatre, and like anybody I also enjoy a
good take away, and a great movie!

Do you enjoy doing what you do?
Absolutely, from the age of thirteen I have been giving out readings
and messages to people, so have not known anything different.
Passing on what I know, to those who are interested, is something
which I can honestly say I love doing, and I will continue to do all the
time I can and Tommy allows me to.

I hope this chapter has been able to offer you a general view of me as
a person, my work, as well as the things which I believe in, and that
maybe it has also answered some of those questions people have
always wanted to know.

Whatever your own beliefs and feelings are, you are entitled to them.

Just remember to smile every day, be appreciative for everything that
you have and enjoy living life to it best.

We are living here on earth to have a good time, not necessarily for a
long time.

Chapter Six – Tommy

Now we come to the chapter about Tommy!
The person I am obviously asked the most questions about.

I can truthfully say that this has possibly been the most difficult chapter I have written so far. This is in fact the seventh time I have started to re-write or amend this chapter.
Not because I do not know what I want to put in writing, nor is it because I do not know how to write it, it is because every time I that have started to write or read the pages back to myself, the voice of my forthcoming spirit guide keeps chirping in my ear, with touchy little comments on how I am coming across and offering me alternative words, or better description other than those which I am considering or have already typed about him.

Like I have explained in a previous chapter, my initial early relationship with Tommy was without doubt very slow; it was like learning to walk again, and certainly took one small step at a time. It could also be quite frustrating at times (from my point of view) as I wanted to learn and know everything Tommy had to tell me as soon as possible. I do think to be honest that some of this frustration was because I did not know how long I would be able to communicate with him for, and I really wanted to find out as much as I could in case we parted company.

Considering that I have acknowledged and worked Tommy for quite some time now I do not in reality know a great amount about him as an individual. I have over the course of time been given information about him, by him, and other spirit energies that I have connected with, but I have never actually had a lengthy conversation with Tommy about his life previously he on earth.

"That day will come though" he says!

So what can I tell you about Tommy?

Well I do know for certain from his accent and from information I have ascertained, that he is a Cockney East End, Londoner, ("*a real one*") who at one time in his life had his own fruit and vegetable barrow, or "*Barra*" as he would say, somewhere around the Old Kent Road area of East London.

"It were a lot different then mind ya"

I also know he passed on from this physical life in the late 1940's following the Blitz and World War II, and that he had two daughters. One of his daughters was nicknamed "Nelly" and by all accounts was a very good seamstress.

I know for a fact that Tommy comes from a large family, and that his grandmother was the person who actually brought him and his siblings up, and I also know that she was a total believer in the afterlife, at a time when it was not really spoken about in openly. Tommy met up with her again when he passed to the spirit world, and extraordinarily I can also confirm that he himself wasn't such a believer of anything spiritual when he was on this earth plain!

Tommy, just like me had an accident when he was a child, in which he and one of his brothers obtained some kind of burns injury.

Was this why I met him whilst at the Queen Victoria Hospital, a place famed for helping victims of burns? Something I still question and still await the answer for when the time is right.

Since being in spirit Tommy leant and gained a higher level of awareness and wisdom about the afterlife before he decided to "adopt me" and to walk by my side.

He literally chose, at the time we met during my operation, to give his life of learning in the higher levels of the spirit world to work with me by allowing me to be here now doing what I do, by sharing the information he gives me, and for that I am extremely grateful.

Each year I do learn a little bit more about his life, and although I could possibly take time out to go and research everything about him using the information I already have, it doesn't seem right or fair for me to do so.

Learning from Tommy, slowly as the time goes by suits both of us very well, and I am sure this is all part of the master plan or another big lesson of his.

"Maybe"

The way I see it is, that all the time that I have more to learn about him, the longer he and I can continue to communicate. Maybe when I finally know everything about him, he and I will have accomplished everything we needed to and we will part company.
What a very strange thought, if this did happen, how my life will be without him around? Will I ever receive another main spirit guide?

Tommy is literally with me always, wherever I go, and I can hear and sense his comments all the time 365 days a year, 24 hours a day, 7 days a week.
Sometimes it is just the odd message or quip which he gives me when passing a place, building or person, and other times it is a full blown running commentary, with images, sounds and smells all to interpret and communicate, to the person which he is aiming them at.

I do not really ever switch off completely from him, not even when trying to sleep.
Although over the years I have noticed, that when I am walking along or sitting resting on the beach, I have no or very little communication with him.
I believe the reason for this is because twice a day the tide regularly washes away all the residual energy from the beaches, consequently cleansing the stones and sand .So whilst walking along on the beach I can, and do get a little short break.
It is quite lucky then that we live by the sea in East Sussex.

Whenever Tommy does communicate with me I can always feel him approaching me from the right hand side, as he has always done from the very first interaction during my operation.
He communicates by "speaking" words "into" my right ear, a little bit like someone whispering in your ear; although it is spoken just inside my ear not from externally, and it is not audible to anyone other than me.
The volume of what he is saying to me changes and fluctuates but generally speaking the more urgent the word(s) need to be said the louder it will be.

At the same time as speaking to me he also shows me overlapping images, which he gives me straight into my thoughts; For example; Tommy may show me a picture of a green tick and without him giving me any further information at all, I instantly know and recognise that this image means "Yes".

Many images like this have all become second nature to me, as I have been learning them for a long time, so it is just like knowing a second language. Therefore with the right set of images being passed to me from Tommy, in a certain order, means I am able to process them a lot quicker.

Why sometimes Tommy chooses to use images or colours rather than words to speak to me depends on the quantity and quality of material he is giving me.

For example; Tommy receives the information he is supplying to me from many sources, including directly from those people who have passed into his world. These spirit energies, who have a specific message they want to say, often like to "approve" the information which Tommy gives to me, to ensure that I am giving out the correct details at the correct time.

Depending on their own ability, some spirits are stronger or quicker at getting across what they want to say, and some are slower, so Tommy chooses a mixture of words, images and colours to give me so that I can differentiate each message, as individual parts of it are given out.

Originally Tommy was the only one actually doing the communication with the other spirits, and he would pass the message to me, I was just his mouthpiece.

But slowly over time he taught me to feel and connect with the spirit energies directly, he showed me how I could gain their confidence so that I can speak straight to them and then receive their replies the same way he communicates with me. But most spirits do still prefer to pass the image through Tommy as they know he has a better understanding of how to give me the information.

Tommy is constantly passing evidence and data to me, as well as overlaying it with sounds, smells and emotions.

Making sure I have all of the information obtainable certainly does help me to complete the picture or account which I am portraying to someone.

But all of this interaction between us happens very quickly and sometimes Tommy can be onto a second thing whilst I am still finishing the first, so it is not surprising that from time to time communications and messages do overlap each other, and can become a little confusing, or they are out of chronological order.

Working with Tommy can be very draining, as I am doing all I can to process all of his information as quickly as possible, and very often I am repeating it to a person or group of people in front of me.
It is at this time when I have to adopt what I and many mediums call "filtering" especially if there are too many images at once or if the details are unusual or unfamiliar.

Let me try and explain to you how filtering works; if you are in the living room of your house listening intently to the television programme you love, and in the kitchen someone has the radio on, when the TV goes to a commercial break, if the song on the radio is one you like, you can switch your hearing from the TV to the radio to listen to it. Even though the radio was on all the time, you only heard it when you wanted too. When your programme returns after the commercial break you switch back to listening to that.

This is just like the filtering I do with Tommy. Some of the background information or messages he is passing to me constantly I do not listen to, as I know if there is something urgent or important he wants me to hear his tone changes and the images become much stronger.

Tommy or "Tommo" as I call him on occasions, has a real loveable rogue mannerism about him, and his broad cockney accent can quite often have a sarcastic streak to it, but in a fun way.
He genuinely looks out for me as well as teaches and guides me in understanding the world as we know it. He explains why things happen, and how they are different in his world.
He teaches me about working with all the energy around me, and about living my life to the fullest and in a positive way.

Tommy also has a fun side; on odd occasions rather than giving me the usual images or words that I am used to, he will give me witty clues to work with, and in the middle of an event this can be quite entertaining.

He also often choses to give people around me very odd nicknames, and then will refer to them as that name for the rest of the event.
He even challenges me by using cockney rhyming slang, such as you can do this on your "Jack Jones" meaning "on your own". Being that I have no knowledge of rhyming slang this can, as you can imagine, also be quite fun on certain occasions!

I have never seen a full clear image of Tommy, just an outlined silhouette figure, which I have only seen on a few special occasions. If I was asked to describe Tommy my own minds eye, just based on the information I know, what I have witnessed, and from his voice.

It would be as follows;
A thin built gentleman, with a certain charm to his cockiness, of average height, in his mid - late 50's, wearing slightly worn clothes including an aged dark suit jacket, with a flat cap over his slightly greying short cropped hair.

"Huh" is a word I have just heard him comment into my ear!

I know from Tommy that my "gift" is just that, a "gift" and I am very honoured to have been given it, and to share it with everyone I meet including you the readers of this book.
To that end I would never abuse the gift I have, and nor would I take advantage of it. I believe that my gift has to been looked after and cared for as you would do anything that you cherish in your life.

I have learnt from Tommy that having this gift is not just all about communicating with those who have passed, he has shown me that energy plays an important part in all our lives and influences how we all feel and interact with each other.
By listening to his teachings, and following his spiritual path I have been able to better my life, and enjoy all that I do, whilst trying to pass this knowledge on to others.

So as you can see, getting to know your spirit guide does and will take time, and it can take even more time to fully understand and appreciate how and why, they are working with you? But when you do make the connection it is certainly worth it.

As well as working with Tommy who is my "main" guide, I have one other spirit guide, who comes close to me, to work with me, and his name is Benjamin, he is a "secondary guide" (Explained later).

Benjamin will always approach me from the left hand side, (the opposite side from Tommy) and his presence is to a great extent much more forceful, than that of Tommy, and I only ever really connect with him when circumstances arises in which I feel the control is being lost, or in a situation where I am being warned that all is not as it seems. So immediately that I see Benjamin I know to automatically be aware of what is happening around me and to check things over again, to ensure I have control. Benjamin is a lot younger than Tommy and he speaks in a very well-spoken highly educated English tone.

It is true to say that a large majority of what I do, is with Tommy's help, connecting loved ones with those who have passed over into their next life, by giving them a one to one personal reading Because being in the afterlife is not a situation we have all faced, nor is it one which we can all yet fully comprehend or understand, with Tommy's help I am able to offer some understanding of what the next life is like.

To a grieving relative who is coming to terms with bereavement "we" (Tommy and I) have on many occasions been able to offer reassurance, support and comfort as well as hard evidence via messages from those loved ones who have passed on, to substantiate and confirm that the end of life on this plain as we know it is not the last.
Life continues on well after departing what we know to be our lives here and now. As you sit here now reading this book I can almost guarantee that someone is around you, and more than likely this will be someone you know personally who is in spirit.

To help explain how Tommy communicates with me I have on the following pages used an actual sample of a reading which I was asked to do for a lady whom I had never met before.

Anne had chosen to come to my home at 9.30am for her reading.

As usual after my morning meditation I was preparing myself for my first visitor of the day. As I was sat down gathering my thoughts I had my usual conversation with Tommy, in which I ask him if he is ready for our day and if there is anything I need to be aware of immediately.

"She's gonna be late", he told me.
He instantly followed this comment by showing me what I know to be a "wedding ring" image.
Asking out to Tommy in my mind, I confirmed that he was indeed talking about Anne, the lady who was due for her reading.
Without saying anything Tommy showed me an image of a "Green Tick" which I know to be a correct or yes answer.
As 9.25am approached I was aware that aside from Tommy, I was not alone.
I could sense the energy of a spirit gentleman in the room as well, standing in the corner just watching me. He observed me for several minutes and I could tell he was slightly on edge, confused or a little unsure about me.
Again, I wanted this confirmed by Tommy, and with another "Green Tick" image from him I knew that I was right.

"It's her old man" Tommy told me, in his cockney way, which I have become accustomed to. *"Dave is his name"*

Allowing Tommy time to try and make some further contact with Dave, I looked at my watch, it was now 09.40am Tommy was right (although I never doubted he wouldn't be) Anne was indeed late for the reading.
Several minutes later at 09.48 Anne did finally arrived, and when I answered the door to her I could see from her eyes she had been crying, although she had done her best to hide it.
I offered Anne a drink and a tissue and we went and sat down.

"It's Dave that she wants to hear from" Tommy Informed me in my ear.

It is at this point in any reading that as a medium that I give my total trust in in Tommy, and I wait for him to offer me the words and guidance on how to approach things, and in which direction the conversation should go.

I started the conversation by asking Anne, if she was sure she was alright, and that she was comfortable about continuing, she nodded in agreement, obviously not wanting to give me any possible clues about why she had booked a reading with me.

Almost straight away Tommy spoke in my ear. *"Let's begin...Dave is new in sprit, he is unsure about all of this"*. I then saw an image from Tommy which I know to be "caution", or "take it gently".

I began to tell Anne that I knew she had come to see me for one specific reason, and that I believed I knew why and what that was. I explained openly to her that everything I was going to say I believed 100% in, and that the messages I hear are given to me from Tommy, and that just before she had arrived I had in fact begun to sense things around me, and that I truly believed it was the spirit energy of her recently passed husband.

Immediately Anne began to cry, "Please carry on" she insisted.

I began to feel the atmosphere in the room change *"Dave's in tears too"* Tommy confirmed as I felt the atmosphere in the room sadden. At the same time I felt a sharp pain in my chest.

I looked at Anne and continued. "Anne I have to be honest with you I believe your husband Dave is in the room with us now". Anne was both shocked and amazed. "I know from what Tommy is showing me he passed from a sudden heart attack, and that you were both so in love."
At the same time as talking to Anne, Tommy showed me an Image that made very little sense; in fact I had to (in my mind) ask him several times to repeat the image so I could see it clearer.
It was of a living room and in the corner behind the TV was a big flashing arrow! On the TV in the room was printed the words "HERE BOBO"

Anne broke down again. After a few moments to allow her time to take everything in, she told me that everything I had said was completely true, and that one of the reasons she was late is that she had wanted to bring along with her, her husband's wedding ring in case that would help me to connect with him better.

She also explained that the reason she had been upset was because after getting the ring out ready the night before to bring it with her, she had mislaid or lost it.
Bingo! The image Tommy had given me dropped into place.
"I believe it's behind the TV in your living room" I told Anne. "Well that's what Dave is telling Tommy".

Anne told me that she would look the minute she got home and that she would let me know.
"*I already know*" Tommy said
"I only have one question that I would like you to answer if it is at all possible" Anne said reluctantly. "Are you able to tell me the little nickname Dave had for me, only he and I knew it, it was a little pet name we shared just amongst the two of us, when we were alone, and if you said it I would know for sure he was here as you are saying he is?"
Sure I can I answered "Bobo".

Anne jumped up and wrapped her arms around me, she was crying with both tears of joy and sadness.
"That's all I wanted to know...Yes Yes Yes" she said "you have changed my life from this day onwards and I do not know how I could ever repay you!"
"*Find the ring*" Tommy said. So that's what I told her!

Within 10 minutes of leaving Anne called me elated. "I have found it; the ring was exactly where you told me".
Anne now keeps in regular contact with me and once again "we" (Tommy and I) managed to help yet another person.
Yet another big green tick from Tommy.

"Together as one", we have been able to pass on some very memorable and very emotional messages over the years, which in no way could have been known in advance of the reading, cold read or double guessed.
These types of reading can be very emotional but are so fantastic to give to people, watching them as they realise there is a connection and that there is something else after this life.

Every time I am able to give such information to people, it reiterates to me how lucky I am not only to have this gift but, how lucky I am to have Tommy around me, this is further enhanced when I receive letters and messages of thanks not just to me, but to Tommy.

I hope that from this chapter you can see how the relationship between Tommy and I works. I am the first to admit that it is an odd situation to be in, but it is one which I no longer try to hide or deny. A long time ago when I realised everything Tommy was telling was correct and that it made a huge difference to people lives, I stopped worrying about what people may think of me, and dedicated my time in helping as many people as possible.

I do consider myself very lucky in many ways to have been acquainted with Tommy at such a young age, because I have had so much time to learn from him, and in truth I am still learning from him, even today. Later in this book I am going to try and explain to you how you too can connect with your own spirit guides, so that you too can learn what a difference it can make.

I know that whatever anyone may wish to think or say, Tommy is real and his is certainly a large part of my life, and I am grateful, lucky and honoured to know him, and I am even happier that finally we have got to the end of this chapter, eventually!

"Eventually!"

We really are "Together as one"!

Chapter Seven – Before you begin your own journey

In my quest with writing this book I truly aim, and hope, to give you, the reader a better understanding from a psychic mediums viewpoint of what is actually going on around you, in fact around all of us, and how we can all connect with it should we wish to? Not just spirits, but all of the energy that is around us in general.

I believe that connecting with energy, the earth, and yourself can bring great rewards, and can help not only better your own life, but those around you who you come into contact with.
So that then in turn, they will subsequently then pass it on to those who they meet.
Spreading the word and showing others how to understand spiritualism, as well as being positive in life, with everyone working together, in a better country, and in an improved world can only be a benefit to all of us.
It is possible, for all of us to live a more enhanced and fulfilled life it just depends on how much people (we) want it.
Rather than a few people trying to change the world immediately, perhaps a better starting place is that we all collectively start with looking at the way in which we view the world, and each other!

I am not by any means at all claiming that this book is going to make you a better psychic or sensitive, nor that it is going to change the world in which we all live in, but what I do guarantee is that you will learn new qualities and attributes, needed to understand, use, value, and better your personal ability to connect with and enjoy, all the different energy around you, which can help to make a difference to your life, if you so desire.

Some of the things I (we) will explain to you briefly in this book, can and will have immediate effect, and some will not.

Many of the things mentioned you will need practice to get right, and a lot of patience to evolve, and even if you think you already know everything remember "practice makes perfect" so keep on going. Even I am still learning up to today.

Never let your belief in spirituality slump. I more than anyone can completely understand when people who want to have and develop this gift find it so frustrating that it doesn't just happen overnight, but the truth is it will not and you do need time to work on it.

Just like learning to play a musical instrument, you cannot expect to pick it up and immediately start playing tunes.

Psychics or Sensitive's are people who are able to sense when spirits or spirit energy is around them, some psychics hear things (clairaudient), some see things (clairvoyant) and many just sense things around them or in their aura (clairsentient).

Mediums however are a channel or conduit for those in the "other world" or "after life" to speak to, and through.

Mediums should without doubt be able to give clear, accurate messages or validations to loved ones still on our living plain from those who have passed on. I class myself as a Psychic Medium, as I am able to receive messages from Tommy as well as sense what is around me at the same time. Remember all mediums are psychic, but not all psychics are mediums!

It really doesn't matter at all at what level you are able to communicate, feel spirits or the energy around you, as long as you are doing it correctly, and that you understand what is being communicated to you and why, and most importantly, you are doing it with complete respect.

So what makes a good Psychic, and does everyone have the ability to be psychic?

At birth, in the beginning, we are all certainly given the gift of seeing and sensing beyond this humble Earth plain into other dimensions, but as we grow older many people cast this natural ability, this "gift" aside.

More times than ever this is not intentional nor is it planned, but solely due to decisions we have made in our life or our lifestyle, and more often than not it is mostly be due to lack of time we all have.

Let's be honest, now a day's in this nonstop society that we live in, with everything moving faster and faster and people wanting things done quicker and quicker, who really has the spare additional time to sit quietly, reflect, think or analyse what they can sense, or have sensed during any working day? Not many people.

To personally develop your own abilities, you not only need to have the appropriate time to do so, but you also need to be truthfully dedicated and committed to it.
I know dozens of individuals, who have tried over and over to accurately connect with the energies around them, but it never quite happens or it does occasionally but not always, because of the continual time that is required to progress.
After a while they all either slowly give up on trying or they decide change their views and opinions about their spirituality.

As I have always explained to these people, "Rome wasn't built in a day", development of your understanding can't and will not all just happen overnight, and it is very important to stay positive and focussed. Stopping and starting your communication with energy is fine but, each time you do, you will still have to go back to where you left off! So when things do not happen as quickly as you expect keep trying.

True Sensitive's, Psychics, and Mediums are generally speaking, a genuine group of individuals confident in their own knowledge and ability; they are sincere in their patience, persistence and desire to work correctly, positively and appropriately.
They are constantly committed to their intense belief that they can and will make a difference by communicating with the energy around them and with spirit entities in other worlds, and all of them would do anything at all possible, to help prove its existence.

Most are whenever possible, very positive in their own life and look at any negatives as differing types of positive energy.
It is important for them to live their life to its best potential and in a way that that makes them feel defined and comfortable, for their own conscience or Karma.

For over hundreds of years now, mediums and sensitive alike have put up with ridicule, and have been mocked at by non-believers and by the scientific world. However now even more the world of science is starting to take a look at this subject much more seriously, and more in depth, and some things are now slowly starting to be learnt.
Psychics have relentlessly said for many years now that everything has and gives off its own energy, which they are able to feel or sense with their gift, something which now the world of science finally agrees with.

Unfortunately though, a great deal more people than ever before, want to be a part of this "new adventure", and therefore true psychics and mediums are presently outnumbered by people claiming to have a psychic gift.
These people really are harming and hindering the prospect of genuine research finally coming up with some true, accurate answers. It is an unfortunate fact that at this point in time too many self-claimed mediums, sensitive's and psychics are being caught out falsifying their so called abilities, creating a situation which makes it even harder for honest, true spiritualists to be taken seriously.

Now today, even the way psychics can practise has been changed, and legally all including me, have to now by law state that what we do is "for entertainment purposes only" and that it is "our own view, and that should not be taken as correct as it cannot be proven".

Even though I fully agree that regulating mediums and psychics could be a good thing, unfortunately I cannot see any accurate way of doing this acceptably. But I can honestly state to you now that I have never given a message to anyone ever, in all my time of doing readings "just for entertainment purposes only".

If you want to find a "good" medium to give you an accurate reading then I would recommend the follow points to help you ensure you get the best from them.

1. Word of mouth – Go to a medium who is highly recommended.
2. Watch the Medium give a reading to someone else before you commit.

3. Attend a free spiritualist church service and see if a message comes through for you there first.
4. When you are having a reading only answer, "yes", "no" or "I cannot confirm that". Do not give them any other information.
5. Try and maintain a steady posture and facial expressions as many "false" mediums can use body language to "cold read" how you are reacting to what they are saying.
6. Any true medium should be able to give you accurate information or validations about a person in spirit, which they could not have previously, know of or found out about.
7. Remember if you are given a message try to wait before you react in case the message has not been completely finished.

How can I prove to you that a message, which I state, was given to me by Tommy was actually from Tommy and not made up by me?

Well surely if the message I give out is totally correct and specific enough, and the fact that nobody else other than the receiver knew or could know the answer, is that not proof in its own right?

Nevertheless realistically and honestly the truth is that currently I cannot actually physically prove to anyone that the messages which I say I see, smell, sense or hear are given to me by Tommy.
This is a statement which all non-believers really want to hear, because there is not currently anyway I can prove it!
But eventually I know and believe that one day I, and others like me, will be able to give that proof to people, as my motto goes, "The answer is out there." We just need to find a way of proving it.

Just take a moment to read some of the testimonials on my website and at the end this book and you will see what the people who have come to me actually think.

Maybe one day scientists and psychics can positively stand together and help each other to find a way to prove it, rather than everyone trying to disprove it by mocking their opponents.

When that day comes I really hope I am there to witness it.

The first thing you, the person reading this book, or anyone should appreciate before they begin to make any type of connection or communication is that it is all of this about energy.

Everything about what I do is based around differing types of energy. Understanding the concept of psychic energy becomes simpler once you value the basics laws of physics, which sees all solid objects as manifestation of a vibrating energy. It is now a proven fact that all of us and everything around us has and gives off some type of energy, which can be measured.

Psychic energy is strong, powerful and invisible mental waves, which can travel across and between the '"worlds". It can accomplish things which us human beings can yet only dream of, especially when it is controlled correctly and successfully.

This sounds a bit of an over statement you may think?
However, invisible waves of energy do exist in today's world that we would certainly not have dreamed of or understood years ago, such as, radio waves, electricity, satellite waves, microwaves, x-rays these are all vibrating energy, and all of these are controlled by a primary energy source, and all need a certain amount of control to make them work efficiently and effectively.

The same applies to our own human minds and brains. Your brain is an energy source, which it is known can create, transmit and receive energy waves.
Understanding how to interpret this energy flow (energy transfer) as it is also known, is the key to understanding and having the perception of what is being "broadcast" to you from spirits or the energy in the atmosphere which you are in.
Sometimes psychic energy can fill a room, sometimes an egg cup but either way it is this energy which you need to be able to connect with.

Keeping your own energy balance correct, and protecting your own psychic energy levels, whist understanding all the types of energy around you, truly is the key to psychic awareness.
You will need to know when your own personal energy is low or high and adjust it accordingly, and this is imperative to any type of spirit communication or psychic awareness.

You should never attempt to connect with spirit energies if you are under the influence of alcohol or drugs, and you should always communicate with spirits properly, openly and with the utmost respect.

Remember if you are being negative and abusive you are more likely to attract negative and abusive energy to you.

Some people chose to work this way to get an instant reaction, but believe me negative and malevolent spirits do exist, and they will take and use your energy for their own gain, which can leave you susceptible to their influence, which in turn can be harmful if not dealt with correctly.

"Without a doubt and very importantly remember, negative energy is much stronger than positive energy to control".

Therefore it is important to understand the different types of energy which will be around you, and these can generally be grouped into the following, and all can contain both positive and negative energy.

1. Residual Energy – This is energy which is left behind from anyone or anything that has been in or around the area. For example, it could be energy left in a room from people being in it all day that you may feel when you walk in.
2. Grounded Energy – This is the spirit energy of someone who wants to remain in the location for a particular reason. For example, a home owner who doesn't want to depart from their home.
3. Visitation Energy – This is energy from any source which has decided to frequent the location you are working in, and wanting you to acknowledge it for whatever reason. For example, spiritual energy of a distant relation to someone in the room or a new spirit guides.

All of us every day, depending on how we are feeling, give out many mixed types of energy which enters the room or the place that we are in.

Sometimes we distribute negative energy if we are having an off day, and sometimes we give off positive energy.

All of this energy can be felt by others around you and has an effect on the total energy being massed in a room.

We have all walked into a room, a pub, or a place which we are not familiar with, and have instantly made a judgement about the feel of the place or the people in it, based solely only on the look, the feel and the atmosphere and /or our "gut feeling".

This helps to confirm that the joint energy given off in a room, from the people and the objects in it can tell you a lot about itself without you even asking.

It is this type of "energy transfer" that you will sense when connecting with any energy around you or with spirits.

So the best energy we can all share is the energy filled with happiness and closeness.

Next time you go to enter a room which you are not sure about because you do not know what to expect try and have a positive mind before you go in. Wear a smile and on entering and acknowledge someone with a nod or a grin.

See what a difference you can make just by changing your own energy which in turn changes the energy of those around you. You will be shocked!

Imagine your own personal psychic energy level being like a battery charging symbol similar to the one on your mobile phone, and the more you use it the more you will need to recharge it. The harder you work using your energy the more of it you will use.

First and foremost ensure your own energy level is high before you start working with your psychic awareness or with spirits, and that you don't use it all for the benefit of others.

Not only can your energy become drained very fast, but it can also become quickly contaminated with other people's negative energy, so always take a moment to cleanse and protect your own psychic energy whenever you can.

There are constant opportunities all around you for increasing your energy, you just need to recognise and remember them.

Nature is overflowing with abundant energy sources which can instantly provide you with positivity such as water, rivers, waterfalls, sunshine, plants and forests to name but a few.

Sometimes the sheer intensity of the energy from others around you around you can increase your field of energy, so ensure everyone you work with remains upbeat and positive.

Take regular breaks and time to recharge when working with your guides, energy or spirit, so that you can stay in control of any situation and of your energy level, try not to allow your energy level to drop below half way, as you can and will be caught off guard.

Below I have listed a few of "Tommy's tricks" which I have learnt from him, for helping me to keep my energy levels up when working, and these may be of use to you also.

1. Wearing black as this can easily absorb energy, from those around you, (as long as they are positive as it can also absorb the negative). If working with others, keep the atmosphere light and enjoyable, laughter is a good energy burst

2. Let cold water from a tap, gentle trickle over your hands, with your eyes closed, and imagine it being from a stream at its source. Feel the energy from the water running through your fingers for a few moments.

3. Enormous energy boosts such as lightning strikes can be times when a psychics or sensitive's energy is very quickly charged and when many have their best encounters, (which is how and why the stereotypical image of haunted houses nearly always appears with lightning bolts behind it!)

4. Smile and enjoy the work, just by keeping happy and positive will definitely keep your energy high.

Just as important as being, "charged" before you start any psychic work, is relaxing afterwards by taking time to clear yourself and your mind.

It will more often than not be peacefulness, and reflection which will help relax you the quickest; this also has the effect of freeing up any blocked energy which may have affected you whilst you worked.

Finding what relaxes you personally will be individual to you, but ensure you know how to before you start moving forward with your own development.

Before I start working on any event, course, speech or reading, I consistently take time to have five minutes alone, to ready myself for the task ahead. Just like a pilot does before taking off, I run through my personal check list.
Am I happy with the feelings and energy levels around me?
Is Tommy happy and ready to continue? (I wait for the green tick).
Finally, I take a few moments to charge my own personal energy levels by connecting and grounding with the earth, I think about my family and friends and what they mean to me, and only then I am ready to start.

When working with any large group, I always get as many people as I can to focus their thoughts together at the beginning of the evening. With their eyes closed, I will try and give them images to consider and think about, whilst asking them to be positive and relaxed. This allows everyone in the group to be part of the situation if they wish to, and allows large amounts of positive energy to be opened up within a room or venue. Whilst they are doing this I can look around the group and feel where the differing energies are coming from, both in the group and externally.

After working on an event or a reading I spend a few minutes alone to relax my mind and lower my energy levels down. I will take myself off for a few minutes, and whilst taking slow reflective breaths I begin to slowly relax.

Now after reading this you should have an understanding of energy and how very important is it, now you have to relax yourself and relax your mind, so that your own personal development can move forward.

Chapter Eight –
Meditation and Positive Thought.

"Do not try and skip this chapter".
For centuries, throughout the world, sensitive's, psychics and mediums, all use meditation in some form to relax them, and to help them focus on the energy they will be working with.
I myself believe and know that some type of regular meditation is absolutely vital as part of psychic learning and development; it teaches you to control your thoughts and your mind.
It was one of the first lessons I had to learn from Tommy and it really honestly doesn't take long to get right.

Repeatedly more and more I hear an increasing number of people say that they cannot do it, and I believe there are several reasons for this. So before you try to skip this section as irrelevant to you, or unnecessary, please just read on and bear with me for a few more paragraphs.

I believe there are two main reasons why people no longer want to continue with meditation.

Firstly people are misunderstanding meditation. For some reason over the past few years people have established an idea that each time they attempt meditation they have to go into a deep trance like state and believe that this could take them a long time to get into, which they do not have. They feel if they cannot get this right they will never be able to make any connections.
This certainly is not the case. Meditation does not have to be deep nor does it have to be for a long time, it can just be short, meaningful, and controlled.

Secondly people have yet another perception that they need to remember long complicated layers of a complex story in their mind, which they have to follow exactly each time to meditate correctly. Again this is not the case, you will of course need to focus on certain images to relax your mind, but these, as I explain below can be what you want them to be, and they do not have to be complicated or the same.

It is true that meditation can be hard for some people to do, but with continual practice, as I have seen with the many people I have taught, it does and will become much easier.

Just like driving a car, once you can do it, it will just happen naturally and you will do it without even thinking about it. Once it becomes second nature you will be able to fall in and out of meditation when you need to.

However it is only easy, once you know how to do it, and why you are doing it? So in the following paragraphs I have broken meditation down into three small parts to make it easier to understand and follow.

But first, why meditate?

As I discussed in the previous chapter all psychic awareness is about the energy around us as well as the energy we give off. Connecting with that energy needs, control, relaxation and concentration, so that your mind is ready to receive any information that is being given or sensed. Any initial information you receive will seem quite, distant and quite jumbled until you are able learn how to "filter" the information. So if you want to be able to connect with energies and develop your psychic awareness you will need to meditate.

Before you can start to meditate you need to have a clear mind and allow the time to be able to meditate correctly.

When a person is in a naturally deep relaxed frame of mind, such as just before falling asleep, which psychologists call the "hypnogogic state", connection with spirits is much easier as your concentration is relaxed and you are not thinking of other things.

Therefore do not try and even attempt to meditate if you have a head full of things buzzing around such as things you must do later in the day, or if you're in a rush or hurry to get somewhere, because this will stay foremost on your mind and you will not be able to relax, and in turn you will not be able to meditate.

To begin with you may even have to make time to do meditation until you are able to fully relax. I know this is much easier said than done especially when we all lead very busy lives, but it is important if you want to develop your abilities that you do find or make the time.

For example, if you were told by someone that you had to find 20 minutes each day, for the next 6 weeks to guarantee you a win on the lottery, I know now for certain that you would find the time as you want the end result enough.

Therefore if you want to sense and feel the energies around you and develop your psychic ability, it really does depend on how much you are dedicated to doing it, and how much you actually do want to make this connection happen.

How to meditate.

Once you have found yourself the time to meditate, you will need a place to meditate. This must be a quiet place or spot in which you feel secure and comfortable, it does not have to be a special room or venue, a room at home is fine as long as you know you will not be interrupted by pets, mobile phones, kids or the doorbell, as interruptions will immediately break your concentration.

Part 1.

Sit comfortably, no arms or legs crossed and relax all your muscles. With your eyes open just listen to and take in your current surroundings. Try if possible to make a personal connection with your surroundings and or the world around you. Take in deep breaths of fresh air, listen for natural noises such as birds or rain water and just relax, calm down from your day.

This may sound easy but could take a few tries to get right, so it is no good trying to do it with this book in one hand and a drink in the other thinking you'll have it cracked by the end of the chapter this will not work!

Your aim is literally to just calm yourself and relax your mind, that's all, but can you?

Listen through the natural sounds you hear close to you, and try to let you mind find the sounds on the edge of your hearing range.
Taking deep breaths and listening to your breathing can help you to relax the mind.

Part 2.
When after a few tries, you can easily relax as described in part one, your next goal is; whilst in this relaxed state, think of a time when you have felt content and fulfilled in your life, let the images just come to your mind.
Try and remember all of the emotions, the sounds and the story behind the initial image.
Try not to let your imagination run free just yet, control is the answer at this stage; overplay the thought in your head.
For example; maybe for you a memorable content and happy time was a birthday party or family gathering.
Can you remember who was there?
What smells can you remember?
What conversations did you have and with whom?

"Remember each time you do this exercise note down the thoughts and sounds which help you relax the most, so that you can use these next time, making it quicker to relax".

Do not try and move onto the final stage unless you are able to control the above two situations in a relaxed and calm way.
You will only be kidding yourself, and you will become frustrated when you can't get any further ahead, and then you will give up.

Keep thinking of your final goal, communication and understanding of the energies around you.

Part 3.The Final stage.
As normal get into your relaxed state as learnt in part 1 & 2, but this time once you begin recalling your memories.
Close your eyes.

Leaving your memories to one side, slowly bring your concentration on to your breathing only, relax to its rhythm in your own ears, and take time to slow the rhythm and control your breaths.
Breathing slowly and in a controlled manor is a very important part of meditation.

"Breathing is the first and last thing we do in this life, so having control of it helps us to relax and regulate our emotions".

Once you are confident your breathing is calm and slow gradually allow your any other external image(s) enter your mind.
Anything at all, that enters your brain, just let it all flow in.
Picture every detail about the images you can sense or see, be positive, and include noises and smells if you are able to.
Allow your initial thoughts to grow and expand.
Learn to feel the sense of wellbeing and control you have of your body, your breathing and your mind.
Remember all you can about this feeling.
Continue each time for as long as you feel you want to.

If you are not getting any thought entering your mind, slow down and go back one step.
Try blocking out all external noises by playing a natural sounds CD in the background, which will give you something else to lock on to.

This place is where you need to get too each time that you meditate, so remember the feeling and how to get there. You are not looking for any messages from anyone; you are purely whilst deeply relaxed allowing all images and thoughts to enter and leave your mind freely.

So there it is folk's meditation, pure and simple. See it wasn't all that bad was it? That is it! So there is no reason why you cannot do it.

The more you can practice and slip in and out of this small routine the better you will become at meditation. Don't rush it, it will happen.
Keep working on this relaxation technique which is now your very own meditation cycle, and as time goes by you will see the benefits of stepping in and out of this relaxation, whenever and wherever you can. You will then be able to use it as the base for your connection with your spirit guide(s) or the energy around you.

Meditation is a fantastic way to just relax and unwind. This can be an advantage to the body by reducing stress as well as lowering blood pressure and pulse rate.
So it's even good for you!

Our being is more than just our physical body. We have a complex energy system, comprising of our Aura, and Chakras (energy centres as some people refer to them), and meditation is a good starting point in taking control of this energy.

Once I learnt how very important my meditation process was, I took time working with Tommy on getting it right.
I routinely meditate twice a day, every day once first thing in the morning and again in the early evening.

My morning meditation I use specifically to listen to Tommy. I take on board all of the images or odd words he has given me in my mind, and I remember any feelings and emotions he shows me and then I repeat the messages to myself at least twice over, however small or insignificant they seem at the time. Sometimes I even have to jot them down.
Usually almost once the working day starts, either working on my business, writing this book or preparing for my first private reading of the day, the messages and images Tommy gave me begin to make sense and fall into place, matching almost exactly the way in which my day is panning out.

For example, one morning whilst meditating the first image Tommy placed into my mind was of a large green door, and a vase of roses. Walking into my first reading that day, was through a large green door and the lady I was reading was for introduced herself as Rose.

Tommy would also like at this point for me to tell you of the time on another occasion when one morning he gave me the very clear image of "keys and a clock" several times, not correctly taking the time to process the images I hurriedly walked out of the house leaving my entire set of keys inside the house.
I was locked out of the house and my car for nearly two hours!

I use my evening mediation to top up my energy levels, which by now are usually quite low, from all the energy I have lost or used throughout the day.

I think of family and friends and recall the conversations I have had with them, and I reflect on all the positive messages I have been able to pass on to people during the day.

Once I feel complete and charged I thank Tommy as always for guiding and being around me.

I finish my meditation every day with a small personal prayer of my own words, sending out positive energy and thoughts to those who are ill or bereaved, and or those who may need healing thoughts sent to them for whatever reason, including those who have asked me by letter or email to help them in some way by sending out positive energy.

If you or anyone you know would like to be added to my personal meditation prayer of love and healing, please email all the details to my website, and I will happily add them to my prayers and send them my healing and positive thoughts.

So in this section of the book "we" (Tommy and I) have discussed techniques you need to adopt before you attempt any spirit connection. It is important to keep yourself fresh and positive as well as relaxed. Do not allow any negativity from your day effect you, either deal with it immediately that it arises or let it go over your head for good.

Positivity:

Developing and strengthening positive attitudes and thoughts is something which I loved learning from Tommy and I still do, and I believe that if you keep an open positive mind you are able instil this onto the people that you meet.

If people decide to be negative around you do not let the negativity affect you.

If you implement positivity into your life, it can and will bring productive changes.

I know it sounds almost difficult to believe but with a positive attitude you will begin to see life, and the way you look at the world differently, you will certainly become more enthusiastic and confident about yourself, and it is well worth trying out. What have you got to lose it costs nothing?

Here are some ways which were shown and taught to me by Tommy, which along with your new found meditation, I hope will encourage you to change the way you think, to help gain a better positive attitude;

1. Learn to communicate with people in a different way, rather than saying no, maybe, or I don't want to!
   Try saying instead, I would love to give that a try sometime or I can't at the moment but certainly would like to soon.
   Take time to think more before you speak or answer people. What are you actually being asking you to comment on?
   What do you really think?
   Rather than just agreeing with others on a negative subject which may have managed to wind them up, offer them your own true opinion, not just what you think they want to hear. Be honest and open with people and show them that there may be a positive view on the subject, which they may not be seeing.

2. Try not undertaking or burdening yourself with things that you may not have the time to do to the best of your ability, but offer to help, and support others.
   For example; Rather than doing all you can to make every cake for a cake stall, make a couple of cakes and encourage others to do the same. Even offer to show people how you make yours, so that they could do it next time!

3. Keep in contact with people, every now and again spend a little time contacting your family and friends, especially those in your phone book who you may not contact very regular, just a hello and how are you can make a big difference to those people and to yourself.

Find out what they have been up to; arrange to meet up somewhere new or different.

As a society, we seem to have become disconnected with each other, and many more people suffer from depression or loneliness, and we can all make a true and real difference, just by giving a bit of time or a smile to someone.

The simplest things we do in life can give us the most pleasure!

4. Laugh and have fun. Life is and can be fun, so enjoy every moment of it. Smiling and laughter is a powerful thing and it is infectious so you can spread it on to everyone you come into contact with. Try reading some jokes, or watching a funny film but whatever you do laugh and smile more, you may even find you like it!

5. Try out new things to do with your time so that your life has a mixture and variety, this way you can see more of the world and what is around you. Take the dog for a walk in a different place than normal, visit a museum or place of interest. Visit and rediscover your local library, and read a book you have wanted to read for ages.

6. Find your spirituality. Meet up with others who have developed their spirituality or who are having the same mindful beliefs as you, and share them.

7. Try and exercise more and eat a little more healthily, if you feel good about yourself this is also infectious.

8. Most important of all, find time for yourself. Everybody needs some time to stop and think and to spend time reflecting. "Me time" is something I am always impressing on people, so take some time for a long soak in the bath, or to have an early night, even if you have to book it in your own diary.

"A positive thinker sees the invisible, feels the intangible, and achieves the impossible".

Once you are able to be more positive and when you can relax and meditate regularly and comfortably, connections or communications with a spirit guide(s) or energy around you can, will then start to begin naturally.

You may now already be receiving small messages or images into your mind through your relaxation and meditation. Always keep a mental or written note of these reoccurring messages, words or images as they probably hold a key to unlocking your spirit guide(s).

This is the beginning of learning the "new language" in which your guide will be communicating with you specifically.

Remember even though you may not necessarily be able to hear your guide(s) they can and will always hear you. Keep talking to them in your mind, you heart, or out loud.

Chapter Nine – Finding your own Spirit Guide.

"How can I find my Spirit Guide?"
"Who is my Spirit Guide?"
"Is my Spirit Guide someone I know?"
"Can I have a Spirit guide like you?"
"Can I choose my Spirit Guide?"
"Is my spirit guide a relation of mine?"

I myself more than anyone know how important it is to be connecting with your spirit guide(s), and I can see and appreciate why so many people want to "find" their own guide(s). So I hope in this chapter to be able to at least point you in the right direction of finding out more about your own guide(s) and how you may be able to connect with them and what to expect.

Many people will try once or twice to connect with what they feel is around them, but because they do not get an immediate instantaneous result or answers to which they want to hear, they give up they immediately dismiss the things they are getting as their own thoughts and not relevant.

Everybody whether sceptical or not has one or more spirit guide(s), and therefore everyone can be influenced by them if they want to be. They are with you all of the time from the very beginning of your life, and you will certainly know when you are connecting with them.

It is important to know and remember throughout all your spiritual work or enlightenment that each guide enters your life for a specific purpose and at a specific time, and when they feel it necessary. Most sensitive's, usually have at least one guide with whom they work continuously, prior to others being slowly introduced.

It is a little bit like being at school, where you have a different knowledgeable teacher for each subject to maximise the potential of the student! One guide may help you with feelings and emotions, another with clairaudience or relaxation.

Guides also come in differing "ranks" and "abilities" to allow you to develop at the right time and speed depending on whatever is correct for you. They may also be assigned to you according to your interests, abilities, and the level of your spiritual awareness.

Spirit Guides are spirit souls, who have chosen after a number of incarnations, for whatever reason to remain in "open" spirit in the afterlife, and they can if they wish assist a person in the physical realm with their own personal spiritual development.
This could be a spirit or person who you were connected with in a previous life, or someone you knew in this life time. However more often than not, spirit guides have not had any other connection with the person they chose to "adopt".

There is a difference between you feeling the spirit of a loved one who has passed around you, and a spirit guide who is around you.
Loved ones do not try to connect directly with you all of the time; they allow their presence to be felt and will be around you but, will always allow other guides to help you develop your requirements.
A spirit guide will be felt more frequently and will continually "guide" you with additional information on the subjects which you are seeking answers for.

Tommy spent over three months teaching and explaining to me the following information, about levels of guides, which I have broken down and would now like to share it with you, as "we" hope it will break down walls and barriers for people who get concerned about meeting the correct guides. So here goes.

Initial Guides.
Before you connect with any guides you will need to get yourself into the right frame of mind and meditation.
Only then will you be able to connect with your "Initial guides", these spirit guides are also learning themselves, they are learning to communicate with you!
These kinds of guides tend to enter your life at a time when you are trying to connect through learning, such as following or during your meditations, during development courses or when you're looking for answers to things which are happening in your life.

These spirits could be many years passed over, or recently passed over, but in their world they would have all only recently completed their "complete transition" into a new understanding and level of the afterlife.

They are then able to start learning how to communicate with those people here and now. Like you, those who they have chosen to "adopt". They will now be perfectly qualified to assist you with the journey that you are on.

Many of these "initial guides" although not all, are spirits whom whilst here with us in this life would have been very interested in and possibly believed in spirituality themselves.

Their mannerism is a very positive one and due to the "newness" of their job, they do not always answer you straight away, sometimes they will have to find out the answers to your questions before being able to reply to you. Sometimes these guides will replay a certain time in your life or set of images straight into your head, to assist them in showing you certain circumstances. This in turn can sometimes give you the regular feeling of regular déjà vu.

The most important thing to remember is that these initial guides do not stay around you forever as it is their wish to progress onto yet another higher level themselves, or even maybe another person, just the same as it is your wish to progress and learn more to better yourself. It is however very common for these initial guides to return at differing stages of your development to "check" on your progress.

One thing is certain, before an initial guide ever leaves you they will help you move on to another initial guide or even a "main guide" if they think you are ready for the next stage, or more importantly if you deserve it by working for it with them.

You need to show these guides your complete dedication in what you are doing; by trying everything you can to keep regular connections with them, such as regular meditation and asking them for assistance. You will also need to begin understanding the messages they are giving you, which may not always be words!

On occasions these initial guides can and will place a feeling or emotion on you instead of using words, and you will sense these feelings as a "gut feeling" which we have all felt at some point. Such as when we fell that we should call or contact someone, or when you know for sure that your instinct is telling you something is wrong.

Main Guides.
Finding your own "main" spirit guide certainly doesn't come easy; it will definitely need hard work and dedication from both you and your "initial" guide(s) to succeed correctly.

"Main Guides" are just like Tommy, a guide who will at some point for whatever reason will decide to connect with you on an advanced level, and they will remain with you as your overall spirit guide or mentor constantly.

These main guide(s) are advanced teachers from the afterlife, and would have specifically chosen to stay and be with you, rather than to continue a life of "full completion" in the open spirit world.
These spirits would have learnt a great deal in the afterlife and will wish to demonstration their understanding and knowledge to you, for you to use correctly and to pass on to others. They will also teach you to connect with other spirit energies including family and close friends if required.

"Only main guides will have the experience gained in the afterlife to give you any slight information or insight about someone future".

Every other guide or spirit energy will only be able to communicate information about the past or present situations.

These Main guides will want to work with you at every possible opportunity, and they will give you very direct instruction on what is or is not correct in what you are thinking or saying.
This they will do, like Tommy with images or words which together you will learn to understand, and eventually you will build a "new language" between you, a language with similarities to that shared between Tommy and I.

Secondary Guides.

The final level of Spirit guide are the "secondary guides" these are guides who will also stand strong by your side when you need them most, but will only appear when you require additional understanding of one certain issue or one specific lesson.

These types of guides will assist your "Main Guide", but they do not take over from them. It is also very unlikely that they were connected to each other whilst on our living plain.

These secondary guides specialise in certain subjects, which they would have chosen to advance in, and they will come forward to assist you only should you need them.

As mentioned earlier in this book Benjamin is my secondary guide, and he comes close to me on the left hand side (the opposite side to Tommy) when things seem out of control. He will appear if a very deep negative energy comes close towards me, to protect me, and my energy by offering additional support to Tommy's.

So how do you find and connect with your own guides?

It is very true that some people can and do "find" their main spirit guide first, without having the other initial guides teaching them. However this only normally happens during a traumatic time in their life, such as during life changing operations, major accidents or out of body experiences.

The key reason for main guides being able to connect at these times, generally speaking, arises because the mind of the person having the trauma is in a "different place" to normal.

Rather than their brain being fast moving and active with many thought patterns as normal, they may have very little control over their minds, which may have been slowed down or been damaged.

This quieter tranquil brain activity allows "main spirits" the relaxed, slowed down state which they need to communicate directly with the person. They do this to offer full their support at a time when it is most needed.

Usually the main spirits that come close at these traumatic times are those who the person can recognise by sight or voice, giving them something subconsciously positive and constructive to focus on.
This helps to explain why following a traumatic time or an operation many people can vividly recall sensing or hearing close friends or relatives around them.

So once again it is important before you do try any connection with any type of energy or spirit that you must first, ensure that you get yourself into the final stage of meditation as mentioned in a previous chapters.

Now to the part about connecting with your own guides, a section which many think is going to be the hardest.
Actually finding your first "initial guide", the guide with whom you will make your first connections with, is actually one of the easiest things to do.

When relaxing one day spend some time taking a good long look at your life, everything that you can remember in general.
What actually makes you tick?
What situations seem to have a repeating impression on your life?
Whatever this is will without doubt in some way have a link to who your "initial" guide is.

For example;
I have always since I can remember (even before my accident) loved London, the bright lights, the big city feeling and the buzz feeling that London gives out.
Whenever I was taken there as a child I was engrossed with it, and always wanted to return.
Watching the soldiers on Horse Guards Parade or attending trooping of the colour at Buckingham Palace, which I did as a cub scout actually fuelled my ambition to want to be in the Army.
After my accident everything I did or have done since then seems to revolve around London. I often worked in London, I have regular meetings in London, even one of my best friends from School moved to London! Everything I do or have done throughout my life has a connection to London.

Now learning from Tommy, I know that because he is a true "East End Cockney" that is why this London connection exists.
Every time I went there I was being subliminally nudged, either knowingly or not, by Tommy's excitement that I was there on his home *"manor"*. Somewhere which he personally connects with! Understanding this from Tommy years later, then made me realise that even though I didn't acknowledge him before my accident, Tommy was always already around me, before we actually "met"!

Therefore to find your initial guide you should be looking for a reoccurring situation in your own life to get a starting place.
I know of people who have an interest in World War II, who have Soldiers as their initial guides, and people who collect show memorabilia who have actors or musicians as their guides. So use this information whatever it is, known only by you, as a starting point.

It can and has been argued from sceptics, that because you are looking for a connection in your life, and are making it fit your situation in wanting to have a spirit guide.
However it is my honest full belief and knowledge from Tommy that everyone's "initial" guide(s) does have this type of connection to your life, and they are therefore giving you repeated signals to prove their existence of being around you.

In the same way as when we meet someone we love for the first time, we give them all the correct signals, and constant feelings whenever we see them, to let them know we care and that we want to be with them, and we do this as often as we can. We even do this sometimes when we know they may not be interested.
Well Initial spirits do the same thing, they drop you consistent hints, in expectation that you will make the link and association.
So once you can find a repeating connection in your life, think about what it is telling you, and then use this to enhance the "focus point" of your meditation and connection exercises.

If you collect or find your connection is with artwork, maybe your initial guide is a painter? So start by asking them if they like a certain style of artwork, or if they can show you a picture in your mind as confirmation.

The main focus for you is to open a communication between you and your guide, however slight it may be or seem. Be positive, open and allow the communication to come forward and begin slowly, step by step.

Invite your guide to come closer to you, and try to imagine them in your mind's eye.

Do not panic or worry if you cannot picture your guide, to begin with just use the initial image that comes to you at this point, as I do with Tommy, and just let your brain run with that image until you are shown or taught differently by them or other guides who will soon come to assist you with correct information.

Connection with your Initial guide is as much a learning curve for them, just as much as it is for you.

Sometimes communication with your guides can be difficult, because our Spirit Guides are working on a much higher vibration, and a higher frequency than us.

"Using meditation you can raise or lower your own vibration and frequency to better match that of your spirit guides".

Too many people think that in order to have this kind of contact with their initial spirit guides that they must hear their voice, but this really is not the case.

There are other ways of communicating with spirit guides. If the psychic gift you are developing is not clairaudient but clairsentient then you may just feel the answers rather than hearing them.

I know many psychics who are not able to hear their guides directly, but can feel from emotions and awareness of the atmosphere around them what they are being told.

Connecting with spirit guides can take many forms, therefore, allow yourself to be completely open to them all, including but not limited to clairvoyance, clairaudience, clairsentience, visible energy forms, dream messages, a spirits physical presence and even a physical movement of an object.

Once you finally make and realise this absolute connection with your initial guides does exist you will feel fulfilled in your mind.

134

Do not try and go to fast and do not to worry about your "initial" guides, they will never overtake you in what you desire to know, you will always be in control, as they also want you to see and feel the connection which you now share.
They will be there ready and waiting to work with you, whenever you want them to.
Just trust your feelings, and listen to your heart. You will know when a connection has happened and when it is just your subconscious talking to you; the difference will become very obvious.

Talk to your guide for a few minutes each time you connect, tell him or her how glad you are to finally connect with them and how you are looking forward to working with them. Get used to how this connection feels.

Once you have communicated with your guide(s) for just a few minutes, make sure you remember to thank them for coming and for being around you. "Respect" is the keyword here, if you want to keep the connection going.

Try to keep your communication slow and short in the beginning, try not to bombard your guide with too many questions, expecting answers to everything immediately, trust me I've been there and it does not work!
Now you have come this far do not run before you can walk, and don't give up if you're not getting the answers straight away to questions you ask, just ask small questions and wait for confirmation answers.

I did and still do this with Tommy to ensure I have a strong connection with him. For example I ask "Is today Friday?", "are you ready to show me images?" and I wait for a reply as confirmation.
Otherwise if you ask too many questions you could find that suddenly you will get all the answers back all at once and then they will not make any sense either. I've been there too!

With Tommy's Help below I have listed a three questions which "we" are sure will help get you an answer to from your initial guides; they are very basic but so is learning any new language.

Do I know you?
Have you ever helped me before?
Are you my only spirit guide?

"If you only expect a simple Yes / No answer, then anything else you may get will be a bonus".

All of a sudden by taking it slow, you will be able to slip into a regular connection it with your initial guides and it will become second nature just like your meditation. Then and only then should you move on to slightly more defined questioning such as;

Was it you who ………?
Can you confirm to me you name is…..?

Remember, you may not get the answer straight away, it may come to you when your least expecting it.

Spirit Guides are around to help, serve and guide us. They will never force you to work, but they will congratulate you in your progress forward as and when it happens. They are kind, considerate and caring and want what is best for you.
They can and will help and guide you but ultimately it is up to you to decide if you want this to continue. You can at any point stop the connections and over a course of time the guide will move away from you.

Congratulations!
Finding your initial spirit guide is a wonderful and amazing accomplishment, I have seen the changes in so many people I have helped get to this stage and it really is a positive one.

Now you have begun, continue to build on your "new language" and relationship and most importantly develop it and enjoy it.

Remember even though you may not necessarily be able to hear your guide(s) they can and will always hear you. Keep talking to them in your mind, you heart, or out loud.

In the beginning if and when the guide is going to speak to you will be their choice, normally it will be very quietly, sometimes quieter than a whisper.

Do whatever you feel they are guiding you to do. Listen to them, and begin to react to what they are telling you.

Remember though this will take time. Do not strain to hear something that may not be there, and certainly do not make up an answer you want to get, just relax and listen to what is being said or shown to you. It will come!

Chapter Ten - Moving Forward

Now you have finally found your guide(s), and you know there is some kind of connection happening, however small, it can very tempting to try run before you can walk, but take things slowly. Just go with the flow; it will get easier, and will be fun.

Just keep repeating the same exercises of positive thought, living life to its fullest and meditating, which by now you will be able to do easily, until your guide(s) tell or instruct you otherwise.
If you respect and believe in your guide(s), they will respect you and enhance your development quicker.

"It is only through constant working with your guides that you can begin to know what they are actually telling you".

Remember your guides are not just around you to pass on information from people who have passed over; they can and will also teach you to understand how and why things happen. Such as explaining the afterlife, and teaching you about all aspects of how to use your gift effectively, which will include how to use the energy around you so that you can help others physically, mentally and spiritually.

So what's next?

Now that your gift is beginning to open up and you are developing your psychic ability from this point forward you can decide;

What do you want to do with it?
What do you personally want from it?
How are you going to use it?
Have you got the time to dedicate to it?

By now, choosing when to use your gift should, not really be an option. You should want to use it as much as possible, whenever you can.

You should be trying to develop your knowledge of what your guides are telling you, and what direction are they pointing you in and what the next steps are which they would like you to take?

"Use your guide(s) as a tool to assist you every part of the way".

Several people come to me and tell me that they have done all of the exercises in this book and that they are actively meditating and they know that they are receiving messages from spirit guides already, but for whatever reason they do not feel that they are moving any further forward from that point. They say they just seem "stuck" and not able to get any further than "off the starting block"

It is at this stage that most people start to lose faith not only in their abilities, but also in their guides and they become stagnant, and more often than not they finally give up.
This is such a shame after coming so far, which is why from the outset I have time and time again explained and repeated to you, this is not going to happen overnight. If you really want this gift you are going to have to earn it, and that is going to take some time.

When people are at this junction it is more than likely that they are just simply not connecting with the correct guide, at that particular moment in time, or that a previous "lesson" which was shown by them has not been fully completed and may need to be revisited before they can allow you to move forward to the next stage.

So my initial advice to anyone who finds themselves at this juncture is to just "STOP", take a small step backwards and review what you have already learnt.
Is there something you have missed, or thought you understood fully but maybe you didn't?
Never should you feel that going over the things another time is going backwards, totally the opposite in fact. Practise makes perfect!

Just as in this life things change and move forward, and we find a different ways of doing things. Well so do spirit guides!
So continual reviewing and reflection on what and how you are working is a good thing.

140

From talking to many people I know that many individuals prefer to progress their own personal connections in a small development circle or group with other like-minded beginners.

I personally agree that this is a better way to advance, as long as you are confident that the circle you are in is being run correctly and that the person or people leading the development group are knowledgeable enough to do so.

The advantages of learning with others include; giving you the opportunity to listen and ask questions of each other, and together you can share your experiences and learn from them.

It can be truly amazing when like-minded people just sit in a controlled environment and are given time to chat, as it can become apparent very quickly, that experiences people share, have many similarities.

What they are actually doing is working in time with each other, and this type of "positive synchronicity" whist working with spirit and energy has a great effect.

If you do decide to join any type of development group, it is very important to ensure you are in a group with people at the same stage of ability as yourself. There are many groups out there that mix different stages of ability, and I know of many cases where someone's personal growth and psychic development has been further delayed or even ruined by other group members knocking or dismissing a member's abilities just because they are at a "lower" level of understanding.

Within an appropriately controlled development group you should be guided and educated about energy control and transfer, as well as shown how to use all of the tools possible to assist with spiritual communication. More importantly you should certainly be given plenty options to explore and use them, both alone and in small groups.

Some people need little or no equipment to aide them; others may need the use of some equipment. Both types of people will certainly need assistance from others, or even a little extra time to master something, but everyone should be encouraged.

Like many mediums I am lucky enough to have been shown, taught and learnt, many varying methods of spirit communication as well as how to use all energy to it best advantage .Comparable to most other mediums I also have my favourites, and those which I specialise in.

In my case, all types of crystal energy and card readings are the methods which I prefer to use whenever possible. These are not areas which I knew I was going to be more involved in nor did I choose them, "they" picked me.

After starting to work with energies from the outset, these two methods have just become ways in which I feel most comfortable working with.

So just like me you should take every opportunity you can to learn more and enhance your knowledge on any aspect of spiritual communication and energy awareness, but ensure this is at a pace you are comfortable with and with people you trust.

If you decide to join a development group or circle you should be guided by those running the development group to help you find your own area of expertise.

You will certainly need teaching and guidance from someone with a much more advanced knowledge than yourself, as this person can then also help you to unravel some of the images and messages you may find yourself coming up against and which you may not fully understand.

The people running these groups should also be advanced enough to offer you constructive feedback based on facts and their own experiences, because psychologists who study how people learn, have found that feedback is an essential key to learning. This includes feedback from other class members and people whom you have come into contact with throughout your journey so far.

Just as there are so many ways in which your guides can communicate with you, there are so many different a tools and ways that you can use to help you communicate with spirits, guides and the energy around you.

I would therefore recommend that whenever possible you try to familiarise yourself with some of them and give them a try.

In the next chapter of this book I will list some of the ways you could attempt to make a connection.

As Tommy first showed me, another great tip on moving forward is reading books on subjects such as the afterlife and psychic development this can be one of the best and most informative ways of learning something new, and giving you advice.

At the very least they may even offer you a differing way of looking at a subject from an angle you had not thought of.

Although most of the principals and ways of working are the same for most psychics and mediums, everyone works in a different way with their guide(s), so be prepared to tweak or adjust what you read to fit the way in which you work.

Do not be afraid to ask people questions whatever level they work at. I have personally found by working within this field, that many individuals, including psychic and mediums are afraid to ask each other for help or advice.

It is as if that by asking others for help or advice you are "admitting" that you do not have the same knowledge they do on a certain subjects and that you are therefore less capable.

This really is a stigma which "we" (Tommy and I) strongly believe needs to change, or we are going to continue to have too many *"Jack of all trades, masters of none"* within our field?

Asking others who work in the same field for help or advice, to understand a situation better, is not only healthy it is definitely a faster way to learn and to move forward.

Everyone whatever level they work at should without a doubt want to work together in sharing our combined knowledge and understanding with as many people as possible.

So never be afraid to ask or even question anyone about how they are working or why they do it the way they do. I would go as far to say that if they cannot answer you or give you a valid explanation for their actions, they probably don't know why themselves!

As I said at the beginning of this chapter "it is all about your own self-development", and now you should have some knowledge about how to continue building on the relationship you have started with your guide(s).

Read, learn and educate yourself on as many differing ways of communication as possible and try out as many different ways as you can. Do not think that you have to do them all perfectly your guides will move you forward and explain more as and when they need to.

Hopefully by now in this book "we" have been able to give you some insight into the world of spirit communication including how and why it happens, and all being well you should have at least some understanding of what spirit guides are, how they work, and what they can do for us. You should certainly now understand about the energy which is at work around us consistently, and some of you may even be in communication with your guide(s) and beginning your journey forward.

"Having psychic ability should not be a burden but something you want to and enjoy doing".

In case you are interested further details about attending my own development circles and courses, all available on my website:
www.marcrichardson.co.uk

Chapter Eleven – Methods of communication

Whatever level you feel your ability to communicate with spirit energy is at; there are many ways you can try to make contact with those who have departed from earth. Some of these exercises below can be done alone, but most should be carried out with like-minded people or even in your development group.

However you decide to try them, and before you undertake any kind of communication, you must remember the "golden rules" below;

1. Do your relaxation / meditation exercises first. To prepare your mind and body.
2. Make sure you only start when you are ready to do so. Do not start if you are not 100% ready to in your mind.
3. Mentally protect yourself, and top up your own energy levels before you begin.
4. Begin your sessions with an introduction to the spirits outlining the intentions of your communication.
5. Be respectful to all spirits and others around you at all times.
6. Stop frequently and keep checking all of the above regularly whilst making your connections.
7. When you feel you have finished your session always thank the spirits around you for being there, even if you felt no communication took place.
8. Spend time following your session, relaxing and reviewing the outcome.

If you follow these simple rules you will find your communication will be successful and safe, you may have been able to obtain the answers you have been seeking, and you may not. Do not be disappointed if you feel you were not able to communicate, the spirit energies may wait until your next attempt to connect.

If repeating the exercise does not give you any results, try another, method.

Dreams.

Some initial guides do find it easier to converse with people through their dreams, as this can be the only time that they can get to communicate, when the receiver is completely resting and their mind is not working overtime.
That is why if a person is not necessarily looking for any connection with spirit, a dream can seem to reoccur over and over to them. This shows that a guide is trying to get through to you and tell you "special messages" or even insights into things they wish you to remember.

To be able to understand each individual part of a dream correctly it is a good idea to purchase a readily available dream analysis book from any good bookshop. This will assist you to understand and breakdown all the details you can recall about a specific or reoccurring dream and will show you definitions and meanings about what you dream contained.

A good tip is to have a note pad and pen ready by you bedside for the moment you wake up, to remind you to jot down anything which you can remember. Try if you can to include the time of day the dream seemed to of taken place at, and the emotions that you felt at the time, as these can be significant in many dream analyses.

For this method of communication you do not need any equipment and you don't really even have to do anything. Just ensure that before you go off to sleep your mind is clear of work and the TV program you were just watching. Spend a few minutes just relaxing your body, and drift off. Night!

Automatic Writing.

Automatic writing is a type of telepathy, where you are able to go into a meditative-like relaxation with a pen in your hand, resting on a pad. The method is to allow the flow of spirit energy around you to come close to you, as you relax into a deep meditation.
Hopefully the spirit(s) will come close enough to you, to allow their energy transfer to the pen, thus causing it to write or make marks on the pad.

I have seen some amazing results from this type of communication including people writing in a multilingual tongue, these are people who I personally know had no knowledge of any other languages before starting the exercise.

I have also witnessed signatures which match identically those of family members who had passed over, and I have seen many specific details such as historic dates visually confirmed right in front of me whilst I have asked questions to the energy affecting the person holding the pen.

In order to get this exercise to work correctly, you do have to be able to slip into a very relaxed meditative state but it is certainly worth trying whenever you can.
You need a free flowing pen and a pad of paper.

Glass / Planchette

I have to admit; this method is a widely used method and it does work for many people, but is not a favorite of mine.
I have witnessed some respectable communication from this technique, especially in larger groups of people; however I have probably witnessed just as much non verifiable communication. However, just because it doesn't necessarily work or sit well for me, it could do well for you.

"Remember having knowledge of the things that do not work for you, as well as those that do, is all valuable knowledge".

To undertake this exercise all you need is a glass, nothing special just a standard tumbler style glass and a table (not your best dining room table or a highly polished table because it could get scratched).

Ideally working in a small group of around 4 – 6, everyone sits around a table within reach of the center. Everyone around the table places one finger very gently on the bottom edge of the upturned glass which should be sited in the middle of the table.
Taking it in turns each person should ask a question such as if there is any spirit in the room who wishes to communicate, and if so could they use the energy around the room to move the glass.

149

Spirits again come close and use energy transfer to move the glass.

If the glass starts to move communication may be starting, in answer
to a question that was asked.
(Ensure that you or other members in the group are not inadvertently
pushing the glass, especially whilst changing a sitting position or by
swapping hands on the object).

Once communication begins, allow the person whose question was
answered as the glass began moving, to continue asking out further
questions. Make sure that you leave long enough gaps between your
questions so that spirits can gather the energy to reply.

Use questions which can be answered by a movement such as "can
you move the glass towards the door for a yes answer and away from
it for a no"

A similar method as the glass, in the same situation, is by using a pen
and planchette placed on paper.

A planchette is an object of varying shapes, which has small ball
bearing wheels on its underneath, and a place to hold a pen through
its center. This allows the pen nib to move freely under it, therefore
creating marks on the paper, if the object is moved.

Many small groups use these methods as a trial to communicate, as it
usually work better with more people having their hands and energy
on the object being used.

In my opinion you should only attempt these exercises in a group of
people you know you can fully trust, as it can be possible for people to
move the objects without meaning to.

Scrying

Also called or known as crystallomancy, scrying has been a technique
used by psychics and sensitive people for many years.
The focal point of any scrying, is an object with a shiny reflective
surface such as a mirror or crystal ball.

Based on the understanding that the energy around or from us, can be reflected, the idea of scrying is to look deep into the reflective object and gaze at the energy that is being shown back to you.

You may begin by seeing small changes to the area around where you are focusing.
Concentrate, keep relaxed as you have learnt previously, and try to understand the images you are seeing in relation to the question(s) you may be asking.

Often people who attempt scrying describe a kind of fuzziness or clouding of the eyes before they begin to see things clearer, this is normally due to the intense concentration and the eyes becoming more focused on one area.
It is important with this method to literally say what you see, however small or irrelevant it may seem. Normally images are placed one over the other, building an overall picture a layer at a time, so by saying each piece as you see it will help you understand better what is being communicated to you as a whole.

This is a very easy method of attempting communication with Spirit and can be done with any mirror you come across, or even a crystal ball, it does take a lot of time to get right but the information can be very accurate, this method is used by many psychics and mediums.

Group Séance

Probably one of the oldest and most frequently known ways of attempted spirit communication is the group séance.

In this method a group of people come together to share their energy to ask for spiritual connections to happen. Generally one person will control the séance and explain what everyone needs to do.

This method relies heavily on the energy transfer between the group of people holding the séance and the spirit energies within the area and should be led by one person giving out the instructions.

It is very important that the group should hold hands or touch fingers in a circle. Once comfortable and joined together the group should take a moment to relax and visualize their own positive energy moving around the circle collectively in a clockwise direction, and this should not be broken until the person controlling the group says it is OK to do so.

Once everyone in the group feels they are all ready and that the circle is full of positive energy, slowly questions should be asked out, firstly by the person controlling the séance.
Different spirits will communicate with different people, so for a better séance ensure everyone wants to participate, and that you have a good mixture of people, and once the séance is underway allow everyone to ask out.

You can ask for the spirits to communicate either by knocking, moving objects or by talking through a member of the group who may be able to trance.

Once the séance comes to a finish or if everyone is ready to stop, the person running the séance should, thank the spirit energy for being around, and then instruct the group to break the circle of energy by disconnecting their hands such as after the count of three. This also gives any spirit energy time to disconnect from the energy transfer themselves. Breaking the energy suddenly, without closing the circle properly, can cause spirits to be drained of all their own energy which they may also be using to connect with the group.

In the correct situation, and with the right people, this method of communication gives very good results, and has the benefit of being witnessed by everyone in the group.
I have been in many good séances, and do like being in them.
This is one of my favorite exercises in a small group.

Pendulum

Sometimes you may wish or prefer to communicate with energy, on your own rather than in a small group. If so a pendulum can be a good place to start.

Pendulums can be obtained from most crystal or spiritual shops and are not very expensive. There are many differing types, some with crystals on some without. Ensure when you purchase one it is one which feels "correct" for you or gives you a good feeling when you handle it.
It is also possible to use a ring or such object belonging to you, placed on the end of a piece of cotton.

Hold the pendulum chain or sting loosely between your thumb and finger allowing the actual weighted end of the pendulum to be able to swing freely below your hand.
Once the pendulum has settled and come to a complete stop, ask questions to your guides or to the energy around you and allow them to use energy transfer to move the pendulum, this should start slowly and then build momentum.
A good starting point is to ask a negative answered question such as is today Friday (when actually is Saturday) and then a positive answered question, such as is my name …..(Your Name).

This will then help you to distinguish what your Yes and No answers are from the pendulum. Maybe for yes the pendulum with spin clockwise and for no it will spin anti clockwise.
Once you have these you can then begin communication by asking out for answers to other Yes and No questions.

This method of communication is limited to what information it can give you, but can be very reactive for individual people.

However you must be very careful that you do not move your hand, or inadvertently move the pendulum, and it can be tricky keeping still for long periods of time.
Even so it is worth trying out, as it can be a good exercise to help you to focus your mind.

Psychometry

This method of communication can be a great starting point and very good platform in helping you to start reading and giving information to other people.

Psychometry is the art of interpreting and reading the energy or "psychic vibrations" contained in an object.

The idea is that you use an item such as a ring, bracelet or another personal belong, given to you by a person who would like a reading from you.
From the specific item given, you explain and tell what information is being given to you from it.
This will include information given to you from your guides and the energy from the item itself.
You may be able to give out information regarding the history of the object, and those who have handled or been in contact with it.

This method has quite often been used by mediums in cases of missing persons.
But in order to receive clear information, the item should belong to the person who is having the reading or a close relative, and should be an item that is not often handled by too many people.

Depending on your level of awareness and your personal ability this method can be hard to get right, and can take a lot of practice, as there needs to be a very good communication between you and your guide(s) and you need to connect well with energy.

When you are able to connect with an item the results will be very accurate, and the information given will be clear and concise.

Firstly relax, and take the item in your hands.
Move the object around in your palm and your fingers and take in the energy from it.
Wait for a while to allow images or information to come into your mind.
Say the images out loud as you see them, even if they do not seem to make any sense, clearing your mind out of the information you are getting is important so that more information can come forward.
Once you feel you have said everything you can; only then should you try to piece the information together.
Remember the information may possibly be jumbled or mixed, this is likely to be because the item has been handled a lot, and you will be

feeling all of the residual energy from it, as well as the information you are trying to ascertain for the person having the reading.

The best thing about psychometry is that you can practice every day with the things you come across and the things you handle and touch. Try it next time on anything even the next page of this book!

I use Psychometry a lot with Tommy when I am working on events. By physically touching a building or doorway I am able to gain a lot of information very quickly which allows me to know what to expect ahead.

Card readings

This is one of my favorite ways of communicating with spirit, energy and with Tommy.

Due to the increase in many people wanting to know or understand their own future, and the willingness to communicate with spirit energy, there are now many differing card decks available for you to purchase all which have different meanings and offer different specific levels of communication or learning.

Card decks available include angel cards, finding your guide cards, fortune cards, and numerous different Tarot decks.
Tarot cards can be a very accurate in there meanings, however they can be very difficult for beginners to interpret and read.
"Our" suggestion if you are interested in learning Tarot is to research online the many decks available and then go to a reputable spiritual shop and physically handle the cards before you purchase them.

Although I do like to do some of my readings with Tarot cards, my preferred method of card readings would be to use the way I have personally been taught by Tommy from day one, this is the very ancient method of using a regular standard deck of playing cards.

The basis of this technique is very easy to understand as all four suits in the deck have a direct meaning to a part of someone's life.
When doing my readings I always give the person I am reading for a guide breakdown of the meanings of the cards prior to the reading

starting, so that they can not only see what the meanings of the cards are, but so that they are able to follow the reading exactly as it happens.

I prefer this method as it also eliminates the fact that I can or could manipulate the cards to my advantage, which is what I have seen, and has happen to me before.

I would love to sit here now and explain the complete way to read playing cards *"Our"* way, but somehow I know that this will be a completely new chapter, with so much to explain, and Tommy tells me that maybe I should write about the way to do to it in *"another book…!"* Personally I would really like to finish this one first!

However you can begin to work with and connect to your own set of playing cards.
Purchase a deck of cards they do not have to be any specification, just a set of playing cards that you are happy with and feel comfortable holding.
Use them as much as possible; this will help you to grow a personal connection with them.
Ensure that when you have finished with them you put them away safely, so that other people are not able to affect or handle them.

There are many mind and psychic exercises you can do with a standard deck of cards and all of them will help you to train your mind to focus and help you to connect with energy and your cards.

Try placing the deck face down, and in your mind picture a colour, either red or black.
Turn over the top card, where you right?
Keep going through the whole pack focusing on each card as you go, try to connect with the cards, and do not allow your logical mind to take over.
The more and more you attempt this exercise the more you should become better and better at getting it correct.

Another mind exercise using a deck of cards is to; place the cards face down, then remove a random single card from the deck and place it face down across the other side of the table.

Turn the rest of the pack face up and fan them out as quickly as you can.
Scan the rest of the deck very briefly with your eyes and your fingers, and in your mind start thinking of the card that is out of the deck.
Once you have a card set in your mind, call out a card, then look and see if it is the one you have removed.

The reason for this simple exercise is to get you to connect with individual cards mentally and visually, I used to love doing this with Tommy, and still do to this day.

Once you are completely happy that you have made a connection with your cards, test them to ask questions about yourself.
Use Red for Yes, and Black for No.

Am I doing this correctly?
Is my name...? (Your name)

These exercises will help you, along with your guides, to keep experimenting with reading information and connecting with the cards.

Until the next book on how *"we"* do *"our"* card readings anyway!

Crystals and Crystal Energy

This is another subject which I am very interested in and has become a bit of an obsession of mine.
There are many varying crystals available, and all have a differing meanings and different effects which they can do for you on a psychic level.
There are many shops now selling these products, so research where the nearest one to you is and go and check them out.

The best advice I would give anyone is to go into one of these shops, use your intuition and be guided to the stones you feel you are attracted to and buy those.

Once you have done this you can use a book or the internet to find out what these stone's psychic and healing properties are. Believe me this is very addictive and once you start you will not be able to stop!

This is exactly how Tommy taught me about crystals and there energy, and now I have many differing crystals, which I use a lot in my work and workshops.
I have seen people with very long term illnesses or sickness; improve their lives by using the power of crystals.

Certain Crystals should be a foundation part of any development course, as there is a lot you can learn from them. So one thing you can do is collate yourself a "Chakra" set of stones, to help you keep the energy around you and within you balanced.

Yourself

Taking away all of the methods mentioned above, and those which I have not covered, the best tool you can use throughout any of your psychic development is your own body.
From your eyes and your ears right to through to your gut instinct, every part of your body can receive communications with energy as they pass through your Aura.

Remember to use all of your senses, they will let you know what is around you and when.

It is very important to note that if for any reason the energy you are giving off whilst trying out any of these methods is negative, this could lead to negative energy being reflected back at you, and you may not get any or the answers you were looking for, nor will you find the exercises easy.

Keeping a positive and open mind as well as working to the "Golden Rules", and things will become clearer the more you practice.

Do not ask for or entertain negative energy, unless you are with a psychic or medium who you know is able to control the situation correctly. Negative spirit energies only want to use your energy for their benefit.

Chapter Twelve – Some of my experiences

Throughout all these years of working with Tommy, I have been so very lucky to have experienced so many wonderful things, and my life has been changed by having him around.

With him help I have over all this time learnt how to use my gift in so many ways such as healing, personal readings, offering advice, and teaching. All of which have opened up so many opportunities for me to experience so much.

The knowledge of the "special language" which we share has grown over the course of time, as well as our relationship, and trying to explain to you every word, feeling or emotion we share and how it works would take me forever.

In this chapter I would like to share with you some of those experiences, starting with a couple of readings which I have selected as they stand out as memorable ones, and in Italic you will see I have described words or images which Tommy has told or shown me during the reading.

Every one of these readings is completely true, and is described exactly as they happened. Some of the names have been changed to keep the anonymity of those concerned, as all readings carried out by me are always in the strictest of confidence. The usage of any parts of these readings has had the prior consent of those people involved.

Reading for Claire.

Mel was contacted by Claire after I had done a reading for a friend of hers. I was unaware of this when I went to visit her at her home one winter's afternoon. On arrival I was greeted by Claire and I was introduced to a friend who was also present Kate, both of who I had never met before.

We all sat down at her dining room table and began..................

Tommy: *"A lady in spirit, singing". Followed by an image musical notes.*

Me: Claire before we begin I am being instructed by Tommy my guide that someone is here with us now and I know that she is female.

Tommy shows me an Image of a lady holding her throat; this is repeated over and over.

Claire: That would make sense to me.

Tommy: *"Mother", Image of the letter "D"*

Me: My understanding is that this lady had issues with her voice or throat, and that this frustrated her slightly before she passed.

Claire: That is absolutely correct. (Tears welling in her eyes)

Tommy was putting humming tune into my ears "hum hum hummm" which I could not recognize.

Me: Claire I believe this to be your Mother that we have a connection with and that through Tommy she is telling me her name which I understand began with the letter "D". To be perfectly honest with you cannot get any other part of the name just the letter "D".

Claire: That was her name Dee. (Smiling through her tears)

Tommy showed me that Dee was standing close to her daughter, humming a tune that would mean something.

Me: Well I can confirm to you that your mother is certainly here and she is communicating with Tommy, I can also tell you Claire she loves singing although I can only hear her humming currently, and to be honest it is not a tune I recognise.

Claire: That makes complete sense to me Marc, this is honestly amazing.

"The song was changed!" Tommy Tells me. "Hum hum, Karen was involved."

A large emotion of love and thanks is placed onto my shoulders. As well as an image of Dee's passing.

Me: I am being shown images that would lead me to understand there is a song your mother wants me to remind you of and that your friend Karen has something to do with. Possibly as song that was changed or adapted for her funeral?

Claire & Kate: (Gasp from them both......followed by tears of very mixed emotions). That's just impossible! Totally, impossible! Do you know which song?

Tommy: "We'll Meet again" now I can hear him singing it.

Me: I am being told "We'll meet again", and she loves you very much for doing it.

Tommy: Placing a taste of peppermint in my mouth.

Me: Your mother loved peppermint.

Claire's mother Dee had been diagnosed with cancer of the throat. Following a major operation she was left only able to whisper and hum, but was never again able to sing again, something which she really loved. As her condition grew worse Claire would sit at the bedside of her Mum and hum songs, which they had previously sung together.
One such song was "well meet again" which they used to hum together all of the time.
Dee sadly passed away, and at her funeral Claire and Kate requested everyone to hum the tune rather than sing it. Dee loved mints but following one of her last operations was no longer allowed to have them. So Claire and Kate used to put peppermint lip balm on her lips to keep them from drying out!

Claire still keeps in contact with me and continues to tell me how much the reading changed her view on the afterlife.

Reading for John

John contacted Mel to book a reading with me, he was very insistent that he came to me, rather than me go to him. John arrived and his first words were.......

John: Hello, and thank you for seeing me. I would like you to know from the outset, before you say anything, I really do not believe in all this stuff. However I have always wanted to have a reading and after I read an article about you in a magazine and as you are local I decided to call and book a general reading.
It was a spur of the moment decision when I booked, and this morning I nearly decided to cancel. It is my intention to not give you any answers to things that you may say, as I do not want to give you any way of cold reading me, from my body language.

Tommy: "Abroad"
Followed by the image of a flag I didn't know.

Me: Thank you for your honesty John, and I fully appreciate your views, can I just ask you to do two things for me.

John: Yes of course.
Images which entered my head were rapid and fast and I could not understand them. I asked out to Tommy in my head to repeat them slowly to me.

Me: First can I just ask you to be open minded to what I believe and allow me the time to explain the things I say or feel.

John: Certainly, I am not here to mock you, I am interested, and I will listen without interruption.

Tommy: "Military.......No Fear"

Me: Secondly can I ask you to agree to tell me your direct honest thoughts afterwards, as you have done before we have started.

Tommy: "Two of them here"

John: Absolutely I will tell you my thoughts on the whole process, but not until the end.

Tommy: "Explain carefully, follow your heart."
Very heavy emotions were put on me by Tommy and I could feel the pain and anxiety being placed on me.

Me: Thank you John, all I am going to do is tell you the things which I believe I feel or sense and I if there is nothing I will also be honest with you and tell you so.

John: OK

Me: I will begin John. I would like to explain that I receive all of my messages from my spirit guide, Tommy, and the first thing I am being shown by him is that there is a definite military connection. I believe you may have served in or are still currently in the military. From the image I am seeing, which is flag, I am sure this service would have been abroad, although being completely honest John; I do not personally recognise the flag so cannot tell you exactly where this would have been.

John stayed motionless as I spoke to him, he just continued to listen.
Tommy's Images became slower and a series of evens started to unfold,
which I now began to understand.

Me: With the greatest of respect John I am being asked to tell that I am also feeling a very strong connection from "two" of your colleagues that you would have served with, and that they are here with us now in spirit. Both of them John would like me to tell you that they are around you, and that they want to make you aware of their presence, of this I am certain.

Tommy: Placing images in my head, I could sense the full emotions of what had occurred.

Me: I have been shown images of an incident and I feel both of your colleagues did not survive. However I know they are both now comfortable with where they are now, and they really want you to know that.

John: (placed his head in his hands) How? How?....How can you of known that! This is so difficult for me to understand Marc. You are absolutely correct.

Me: I have one final message to you from them.

John: OK?

Me: "It is still your round!"

John: Oh my god! That is truly unbelievable.

Holding back his tears and wrestling with his feelings, John explained the whole situation to me. The incident was indeed in Iraq, which killed his two colleagues instantly. The last conversation they had shared was about whose round it would be the next time they eventually ever get home to the pub, something which had been a long standing joke between the three friends.
John was true to his word and after the reading had ended, and he told me that he was never expecting to hear the information I gave him so accurately. He also explained that he could not quite understand it or how it happens, but however it does; he now knows it is possible.

Readings, like the two you have just read, do not always happen like that nor are they always so detailed, sometimes the information comes in waves and very fast, so interpreting it can be harder.

As a medium I am very conscious that people I read for want to hear specific details as verification that their loved ones are around them, and those are the messages I want to give.

However sometimes those in spirit are giving out differing messages other than those that the person having the reading wants to hear.

166

On occasions when I sit ready to read for someone, I can hear several differing spirits calling to Tommy; I have to wait for him to understand what is being said, before he can filter it to me and I can pass it on.

Sometimes it really can be a little bit like "Chinese whispers" as things are not clear or I have misheard or miss read what I have been given.
I admit here and now in writing I make mistakes, but I never lie.
I will only tell someone the things you have definitely heard, felt, received or I believe I have been guided to say.
I never elongate any answer by filling it out with gobbledygook or by making up your own interpretations from small pieces of information. I say it exactly as I believe I am getting it.
Honesty in all cases really is the best and only policy.

On one very funny occasion, I totally miss-read an image from Tommy; I was working an event in London at a very famous location. As I was walking around the premises I stopped and turned to the historian.....

"I am very clearly hearing cups and saucers" I told her "and I feel that this area would have been a tea room."
"Correct!" said the lady historian "Do you know the name at all"
Asking out to Tommy in my mind, I asked if he could give me this information. I immediate saw a quick flash image of what I thought was a picture of a tiger. Asking Tommy to repeat the image again, I did see a rough outline of the head of what I was sure was a sketch of a "tiger".
"Tiger Tea Rooms" I announced out loud to everyone watching and listening, as I described what Tommy had shown me from his sketched image.
"No you are wrong sorry" said the historian laughing "very near but not quite!"
"Lyons Tea Rooms" She said "A lions face is a bit like a tigers though!"
Even I laughed and saw the funny side, and I jokingly I asked Tommy not to sketch his own images again!

Some of the experiences I have had have whilst doing readings or events have been unique and very special, some have been fun and made me laugh so much, and others have been quite emotional and I thought I would share some of my favourite experiences with you now.

Ghost Buster Man

Once I turned up on a paranormal event and on being introduced I entered the room where everyone was sitting waiting to begin.
In the corner of the room I could see one person who made himself very noticeable, as he jumped up to greet me.
He had come along all prepared for the evening in his comprehensively hired "Ghostbusters" costume, complete with all the apparatus strapped to his back!
This certainly did made me laugh, and would not have been as fun, if he was not completely drunk, and fell asleep 30 minutes into the investigation, after telling me and all of his friends how he was single handed going to save us all from the ghosts!

Crying Rugby Players

During a final vigil late one night at Newhaven Fort, in East Sussex, I was running a group with several people in it who included two very large rugby playing brothers.
These two guys I think it would be fair to say had been very uninterested in what was happening all evening. They were certainly sceptical about the world of the paranormal, but wanted to wait around for the final vigil which would be with me, to see if anything would change their opinion. The vigil was to be held deep within the forts caponier.
We began the vigil by sitting on chairs in a circle, and as I was talking to the group Tommy made me aware of a dark image walking down the corridor about 50 feet from where we were sitting. I told the group about the image Tommy was showing me and without a thought the two brothers starting shouting out.
"Come on then, come to us now we don't care, prove you're here."

I tried twice to explain to the guys that I will only work with respectful people and that I wished them to refrain from shouting such comments.

I asked the group to sit quietly, and to continue holding hands whatever occurred, I spoke through Tommy, to the energy which was now standing only a few feet from us, asking the gentleman spirit who was there if he would like to join us in the room.

Before I had time to explain to the group that this gentleman was now with us the two brothers starting whispering to each other, arguing about which one was rocking the other ones chair.

Their voices increased with absolute fear, as both of them realised from the small amount of light in the room, that nobody in the room was touching their chairs.

"What is going on?" asked one of the men as the chairs continued to rock violently, "stop this now, please stop this Marc"

Again through Tommy I spoke to the gentleman who was now affecting the rugby player's chairs and asked him to please step back away from them.

"He is going to go, Tommy told me, but first......"

Without warning both brothers shot up from their chairs, still holding hands with the people next to them, as the gentleman walked directly out of the room and right through them.

Regaining control of the room I requested that slowly the group counted from 10 backwards before letting go of each other's hands.

As soon as hands were released the two brothers literally ran from the room and ascended the 60+ plus steps out of the caponier. A few minutes later they were both found outside sharing a cigarette and wiping tears from their eyes.

Coffee Shop Chaos

I have ended up giving readings and messages to people who never even expected it, such as the time I was sitting with a friend in a coffee shop, when the waitress came over, my friend who finds what I do to be "interesting" suddenly came out with

"He's a medium! Are you a believer?"

I spent the next 25 minutes, with Tommy's help, giving the lady a mini reading and messages from her sister who was in spirit as well as an aunt. What started as two of us having a quick cuppa, ended in three of us having lunch!

Getting the language right.

On another occasion Mel was contacted by a lady who had seen a magazine article about me, she requested and booked a reading with Mel and it was agreed that I would go to her home on the next available date a few weeks later.

I arrived at the "Tina's" home and following a cup of coffee we began her reading.

All of a sudden I was unable to hear Tommy correctly, he was talking gibberish and nothing was clear.

I apologised to Tina and told her that everything I was hearing was sounding odd from Tommy.

I began to try and repeat out loud phonetically all of the things Tommy was saying to me.

I understand everything what you are saying Tina said, your words are in Spanish and my best friend who you have made contact with is Spanish! This had never happened to me before, as normally when Tommy speaks to me he speaks in English. Even on the occasions where I have had foreign Christian names or places to say Tommy would usually give them to me phonetically to repeat, never before had the words and complete sentences all been in one language.

They have spelt my name wrong.

Sometimes I have even been put in the position of telling people here on our plain in the living now, that they are wrong!

Whilst on another event one evening, I was wandering around with a couple of people just taking in the atmosphere of the venue and looking at all the artefacts that were on display.

We walked passed a cabinet which contained copies of people's old driving licences.

Stopping to look I heard Tommy say to me that someone was in the room and had something they wanted to say.

"They have spelt my name wrong" said a voice in my ear.

"Look there on the red book" Tommy said

I studied the only little red book in the cabinet which had printed on the front Mr R T Smyth; in slightly warn out ink pen handwriting.

"Look on the card above" Tommy told me

As I read the description card placed inside the cabinet along with all the objects on it, it read; ....and also a small red post war driving licence belonging to a Mr R T Smith.!
Mr Smyth, and Tommy were right, the name had been spelt wrongly.
I spoke to a member of the staff at the venue and explained the situation.
They very happily changed the name on the description card, especially when I explain who had pointed it out to me!

Intercom Interference.

Walking through the passageways of a fort one evening I was explaining to the people with me what I could feel and sense, this included me telling them that a very large force was trying to say something to us.
I asked everyone to stop walking, stand still and to join hands to give out more energy.
As we did this the location PA system started to crackle and mumble noises.
Suddenly an angry voice could be heard, making most people jump.
"That was a negative spirit" Tommy told me
Ending this vigil, I and several of the team members who were running the event went off to speak to the venue manager, to see if it was him who was trying to speak to us via the crackling speakers.
When we arrived at his office and asked him he looked a little shocked.
That PA system is off, if fact it is unplugged every evening he told us, to confirm he took us to the locked cupboard the system was held in.
He unlocked it and showed us the plug which was certainly not in the socket.
During the final vigil of that same evening the entire group was again in the dark tunnels and we were talking about what the evening had been like for us all.
Whilst discussing what we had experienced, we heard whistling, and a few loud bangs making a few people jump.
This you may think was enough to make anyone to jump, but when the unplugged PA system again shot into action mumbling and cracking, a voice appeared to say LEAVE.

I knew where I was...

Doing individual private readings for people all over the UK and Europe, I have felt so many vast emotions that I could never ever really describe them all to you, such as the time I first met Tommy.
However nothing could have touched my emotions and heightened my awareness as the specific day I found myself literally mentally torn apart with emotion.

As I stood facing forward, looking into the distance, with the buildings standing tall around me, I was trying to find something individual to focus my mind and my eyes on.
I could feel the continuous wave of energy flooding towards me, I felt the fear and the sadness that Tommy was showing and placing on me, and my stomach churned over and over.
So many messages were coming into my mind, and so fast, I couldn't take any of them in or interpret them.
Trying to recover my composure I attempted to look away from the direction which all of the energies were coming from towards me to, but I just couldn't.
Tommy kept asking me to receive the images, and take as much of them in as I possibly could.
As I did I couldn't help it, I began to feel my eyes welling up, and I had to stop.
Listening to the noises and voices around me, I could feel my personal energy beginning to drain from me so fast.
As I stood there with tears running down my cheek, I will never forget my visit to "Ground Zero" New York, where I went to pay my personal respects to all those who had lost their lives 9 years earlier.

Rest in Peace x

Chapter Thirteen – Past, present and the future.

Since my accident in 1983, my life began again in a very special way and now almost 30 years later, I have reached the end of this my first book, which in theory has taken me just as long to learn and understand before it could actually be written.

Throughout all of those years I have been able to walk around on my injured foot which the surgeons so carefully reconstructed for me. Although it is true to say that every day since the accident I do suffer with a lot pain, most of it I have learnt to block out mentally.
There are the odd days when I know I have over done it on that foot, as my limp begins to return; but generally I feel that I have done really well, and my injury has never stopped me doing anything.

Constantly working on my business, paranormal events, personal development courses as well as all the readings I do, certainly keeps me busy, but it also means that I have been honored to meet so many wonderful people who I have been able to share my gift and knowledge with, and I look forward to meeting so many more in the future.

Working as a medium can and has certainly be challenging at times, throughout my career so far I have witness and heard so many differing opinions from both sceptics and believers, and just as I think I have heard every argument for and against what I believe in, someone will come up with a new approach which they want to quiz me about, but I find this healthy.

I have nothing to prove or hide from anyone; I just do what I do because I am lucky enough to be able to do so, and I believe in it 100%.
I do not seek extreme fame or fortune for doing it; I truly just enjoy it, and know I have a path to follow.

I do hope that within my life time on this earth, more of what I and other mediums say can become more verified, and I look forward to a day when everyone can learn that by living and working together positively, we can all really make a difference to our lives.

To finish this final part of this the final chapter I decided I wanted to share with you some of the very kind words which people have taken the time to write to me.

Some are from people who I have done readings for, and some are from people who I have been on paranormal events with, and I am so grateful to all of them not just for taking the time to write and send them to me in the first instance, but also for allowing me to share them with you.

"By using various methods of which he is both experienced and very knowledgeable in, Marc Richardson has a real natural gift which must be seen or felt to understand or appreciate..."
July 2010

"I honestly do not know what to say!.....I came to you a total 100% skeptic but had heard so much about you I thought I must come along and try out a reading.....within minutes you not only told me everything about me and my life to date, but you also passed me messages through Tommy from people close to me who have passed over.... These I found to be extraordinarily spot on, your positivity made me think about how I live........Everything you told me made perfect sense and was totally accurate........ All I can say my friend is thank you very much and keep doing what you do".
August 2011

"Coming to you for a regular reading really helps me to stay positive, and reminds me that life is for living to its fullest, thank you and Tommy for helping me"
October 2011

"Every time I watch you work, I see how much of a difference you make to people's lives, your connection with Tommy and your openness and honesty is something which everyone should experience"
December 2011

"The readings I have had with you are always very accurate, intense and always help to focus me on what is important as well as things I need to action to 'get back on track'. Being 'Miss Perfect' means sometimes it's emotional but always helpful. You are an amazing friend to have, and I always look forward to Tommy's sound bites and your advice both personally and spiritually". **January 2012**

"A personal testimony given for a most extraordinary man and the undoubted gifts and abilities he displays when revealing the communication, discussion and knowledge attributed to those no longer with us in this universe . To say that this has disturbed and questioned the way in which I base my life and understanding of certain commonly held beliefs does not begin to describe the point at which I find myself.

My background is that of a scientist for some 45 years with a background in Physics and a Masters in materials science, running high technology businesses, with papers published and lectures given to such as the Russian Academy of Sciences.

The experiences and information provided by Marc during my meetings and readings with him, defied understanding and I could only liken to the strange and difficult events in physics for which revelations of parallel universes and quantum entanglement of particles are now accepted as explanations for events not understood not so many years ago.

At present the scientific community has I commonly accepted that particles can disappear and re-appear having passed into another universe, with the Large Hadron Collider taking us into almost meta-physical events.

Maybe it is time that we should look at the abilities that Marc can display as possibly a further extension of our present day understanding of the meta-physical.

To describe Marc as a psychic medium only raises to those like myself an instant skepticism born of smoke and mirrors which was destroyed completely after the first and subsequent meetings. (Note not readings.) Why did I go? Difficult to say, except that at a difficult and turbulent time in my business and family, my daughter as a Christmas and Birthday present, took me so I could "think of other things".
I have no hesitation in endorsing Marc as to the accuracy, and value for the information he is able to reveal. He deals with his very difficult and complex "psychic ability" with true kindness and patience, especially with those like me who find the whole thing almost unapproachable."
March 2012

"Even without the gift he possesses, Marc would still be the remarkable, honest, trustworthy, kind and empathic man that he is. His spiritual abilities are just an additional blessing. Whenever I have a reading with Marc I may not always hear what it is I think I want to hear, but I know without doubt that the information and guidance he gives me is what I need to hear, no more, no less! I am always astounded by the accuracy of his work both in his readings and when I have been fortunate to join him on paranormal investigations. His is without doubt the best medium I have witnessed, and I feel privileged that I can now call him a friend."
March 2012

By using this book to help you find your inner self, working with the energies and guides that are around you, and by having a positive attitude, I know that you the reader can become a better person, and that this will have a positive lasting effect on the way you live your life as well as those around you.

In principal as a nation and as people, we have the knowledge, awareness, education and understanding to help each other, as well as facilitating a better positive life for everyone just by making a few small changes, but will we? Or will we just continue to walk on past and allow "others" to make the changes "one day in the future"?

Remember;
- Do not give up, keep going and it will happen.
- Meditate regularly
- Keep positive and do not allow negativity from others affect you.
- Finding and having this ability is a true gift, do not abuse it or fake it.
- Ask others for help if you do not understand something, anyone who really cares will help you.
- Treating and talking to people with the same respect you would expect really can move mountains, and will encourage others around you to do the same.
- Respect everyone's view no matter what their colour, sexuality, beliefs or religion.

I cannot tell my own future, so I have no idea as to where my future is currently heading, all I know is that I will continue to do what I do for as long as I can, and as long as my family and friends support me.

There are certainly things which I would like to do in the future, such as investigating and being left locked alone on Alcatraz Island, maybe for charity?

Maybe one day even doing a small tour of the UK giving talks to people, and signing my book!

Wherever my future leads, every word of this book has been written from my heart, and it is my honest and open opinion of what I have experienced and of what I actually believe.

Writing this book has certainly been an amazing journey for me personally, and now that I come to the final pages it all seems quite unreel that I have actually done it, "we" have actually done it.

It would not be right for me to finish this book without thanking all of those who have been a great support to me whilst writing it, especially my wife and children, as I have spent so much time locked away working to complete this dream.

If you have this book in your hand I personally thank you for reading it, and I genuinely hope you have managed to at least gain something from it, however small that may be, and that in some way shape or form, it has been able to give you some awareness of what is actually around us all.

Of course, if you are reading it, then someone somewhere had the faith in me to actually publish it, so to them I also say thank you for helping me realise a dream, and reaffirming to me again that my belief in myself, and in positive thought really does work!

Last of all and most importantly I thank you Tommy, my mentor, my teacher and my friend, without you I would not have been given the chances to see what I have seen, meet the people I have met and nor would I be able to do what you have taught me to do.

I undoubtedly hope our relationship continues for some time yet, and I look forward to the day I actually get to stand by your side, and shake you by the hand.

My final words to all of you are;

Cherish those, who you hold dear in your heart,
Remember with love, those who have passed,
and more importantly, communicate with them all, always. x

For more information about Marc's work:

Facebook: Medium Marc Richardson

Twitter: @Richardsonmarc

Web: www.Marcrichardson.co.uk

Email: Admin@marcrichardson.co.uk